Norse Magic & Runes:

A Guide To The Magic, Rituals, Spells & Meanings of Norse Magick, Mythology & Reading The Elder Futhark Runes

History Brought Alive

© Copyright 2021 - All rights reserved.

The content contained within this book may not be reproduced, duplicated or transmitted without direct written permission from the author or the publisher.

Under no circumstances will any blame or legal responsibility be held against the publisher, or author, for any damages, reparation, or monetary loss due to the information contained within this book, either directly or indirectly.

Legal Notice:

This book is copyright protected. It is only for personal use. You cannot amend, distribute, sell, use, quote or paraphrase any part, or the content within this book, without the consent of the author or publisher.

Disclaimer Notice:

Please note the information contained within this document is for educational and entertainment purposes only. All effort has been executed to present accurate, up to date, reliable, complete information. No warranties of any kind are declared or implied. Readers acknowledge that the author is not engaged in the rendering of legal, financial, medical or professional advice. The content within this book has been derived from various sources.

Please consult a licensed professional before attempting any techniques outlined in this book.

By reading this document, the reader agrees that under no circumstances is the author responsible for any losses, direct or indirect, that are incurred as a result of the use of the information contained within this document, including, but not limited to, errors, omissions, or inaccuracies.

Free Bonus from HBA: Ebook Bundle

Greetings!

First of all, thank you for reading our books. As fellow passionate readers of history and mythology we aim to create the very best books for our readers.

Now, we invite you to join our VIP list. As a welcome gift we offer the History & Mythology Ebook Bundle below for free. Plus you can be the first to receive new books and exclusives! Remember it's 100% free to join.

Simply click the link below to join.

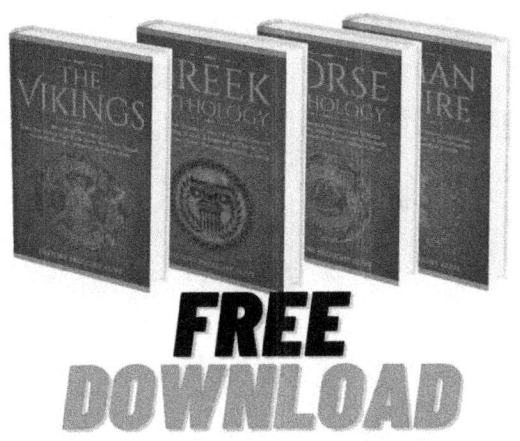

[Click Here For Your Free Bonus (https://www.subscribepage.com/hba)](https://www.subscribepage.com/hba)

Keep upto date with us on:
YouTube: History Brought Alive
Facebook: History Brought Alive
www.historybroughtalive.com

Table of Contents

Introduction 1
   Welcome 3

Chapter 1: The Time & People 8
   More Than Just Norsemen 9
      Daily Life 11
      Slavery 13
      Women 14
   More Than Just Vikings 15
      Different Ventures 17
      Icelandic Settlements 19
      Conflicts and Raids 20
   Their Influence 21
      The Celts 22
      The Norse-Gaels 23

Chapter 2: The Gods & Realms 25
   The Pantheon 26
      The Æsir 27
      The Vanir 33
      The Valkyries 37

- Cosmology 38
  - Nine Realms 40
  - Yggdrasil and the Norns 40
  - Ragnarök 42
- Trolls, Dwarves, Elves, and Giants 42
  - Trolls 43
  - Dwarves 43
  - Elves 44
  - Giants 45

Chapter 3: The Myth & Folklore 46

- The Eddas 49
  - Poetic Edda 50
  - Prose Edda 52
- The Icelandic Sagas 53
- Some Stories and Themes 54
  - Skirnismál: The Lay of Skírnir (Poetic Edda) 55
  - Frithiof's Saga (Legendary Saga by Esaias Tegnér) 59
  - Grímnismál: The Lay of Grímnir (Poetic Edda) 62
  - Skáldskaparmál: The Kidnapping of Idun (Prose Edda) 67

- Scandinavian Folklore 70
  - The Huldra 71
  - The Nisse 72
  - Pesta 73
  - Nokken 74
  - The Draugr 74
- **Chapter 4: Seiðr, Spà, & Galdr 76**
  - Seiðr 78
    - Connection to Shamanism 79
    - Performing 80
    - Derivation 82
  - Spá 84
    - Connection to the Norns 85
    - Performing 86
    - Derivation 87
  - Galdr 88
    - Connection to the Songs 89
    - Performing 89
    - Derivation 91
- **Chapter 5: Runes & Runestones 93**
  - Odin's Gift 96

- Elder Futhark 99
- Younger Futhark 101
- Rune Poems 103
- Icelandic Rune Staves 110
- Runestones 112
  - Tools Used 113
  - Where They Stand 115
  - Reading the Stones 117
  - Runemasters 118

Chapter 6: Runic Divination 120
- The Three Ættir 122
  - The Mother 123
  - The King 125
  - The Warrior 128
- Casting 130
  - The Ætt in Casting 131
- Rune Spreads 132
  - One, Two, and Three-Rune Layouts 133
  - Four-Rune Layout 135
  - Five-Rune Layout 135
  - Seven-Rune Layout 136

24-Rune Layout 138

The Blank Rune 140

Chapter 7: Religion 141

Public and Private Faith 142

Public 142

Private 143

Death & Reincarnation 145

Parts of the Soul 146

The Afterlife 147

Ghosts 148

Sacrifice 148

Chapter 8: Connection to Nature & the Unseen 152

Their Concepts 153

Cyclical View of Time 154

Herbs and Potions 155

Sacred Numbers 157

Spirit Worlds 158

Wights 158

Útiseta 160

Totemism 161

The Fylgjur 162

Militaristic Totemism 163
Chapter 9: Norse Morality & Ethics .. 165
Law 165
Virtues and Values 166
After Conversion 168
Conclusion 171
Farewell 173
Free Bonus from HBA: Ebook Bundle 176
References 178

Introduction

The night is cold and silent. No wind stirs the snow-covered Rowan trees; the only sound is the soft snow footsteps of Bo and his son Arne as they climb slowly up the ridge to the viewpoint above their village, this being a tradition spanning back many moons of old. Bo remembers the times when his father would take him up the same journey to witness the magnificence of the northern lights.

"This was a moment for clarity and presence," he always said. His father enjoyed telling stories while they stood there and watched with awe, in a way to honor and remember their gods and their influence over the men in the world.

Now Arne places his last step before they finally arrive at the leveled area between two Ash trees. He takes his place beside his father as the lights above them stir like ribbons of color dancing and mingling with one another in ridges and sways. The stories Bo tells his son are the same stories his father told him as a young boy—stories of legendary warriors and mischievous trolls, old mysterious seiðmenn, and beautiful, fair queens. But none spoke more to his heart than the story behind the northern lights.

Odin is the chief god of Asgard, and the Valkyries, his faithful embodiments of strength and wisdom, were the women of war who would ride by his side to battle or would collect the souls of fallen men and return them to Valhalla, the hall of the slain. As they rode in the skies, the reflection of light off their mighty shields would illuminate the night sky above their heads, creating the northern lights.

The myths and tales told were not fictional but an honest guideline to every aspect of their lives. Arne knew it to be true, and that was all that mattered.

When they returned home, the house was warm and inviting. The smell of dinner and the loving embrace from Bo's wife, Frida, was the usual evening greeting and always appreciated. Frida was a woman of magic, you see. Arne always understood the need to sit quietly with his mother in the morning and at night to make offerings to the gods for blessings and chant to the spirits for answers—some for Father's health and protection, some for Mother's fertility and strength, and some for Arne's own courage and virility. Daily rituals of worship were led by both his mother and father, and they encompassed the honoring of many gods and goddesses alike.

They were always assured that the gods were with them, even when they closed their eyes.

Welcome

Hello there friend! Welcome to the world of *Norse Magic & Runes*!

Here at History Brought Alive, we like to tell history through the mind of the reader. Meaning that when you come back to this book each day you will bring your mind into the life of a Norseman—breathing, feeling, and smelling their environment around you.

The worldview of these ancient Nordic people was so incredibly different from ours that it can be hard to imagine yourself in their shoes. That is why we take the time and care to transport you to the cold, green hills, plains, and mountains of Scandinavia between the 8th and 12th century.

Your interest in learning about the magic of the ancient people of Scandinavia is saluted! The experience of finding a piece of work that tells a story you can understand, relate to, and be intrigued by all at once is what you desire and deserve; therefore, look no further. *Norse Magic & Runes* will take you right into the heart of their magic and ritual practices.

The varied and complex history of Norse people can become a rather confusing ordeal to get through, considering the large language variants and influences of Christian beliefs in the historical evidence. Many manuscripts find themselves falling quite short of the hope and expectation given by readers interested in the truth behind the mythology and magic of the Nordic people. Often enough they are long-winded and honestly rather boring in their retelling. Instead of having text that just talks at the reader, we want to create a text that allows the reader to immerse themselves in the writing.

We know you cannot wait to learn the ins and outs of the different practices and the language used, but like any journey, we will have to start at the beginning.

We will first look at the people who lived during this time and the lengths to which they went to achieve greatness, because without the creation of a context, the meat of this manuscript would come across empty and lacking in meaning.

Then, we will guide you into the pantheon of the gods and goddesses and the various realms they ruled over. Once we pass over the deities, we can begin with the stunningly elaborate descriptions of the mythologies and folktales filled with heroes, gods, and common people striving to find their truth. These stories hold so much weight that they still reflect in our modern lives today.

And then onto the magic! That's what you have been waiting for, right? The magic arts we delve into are the three main acknowledged and studied forms of magic: seiðr, spá and galdr. Magic is where silence and peace were each an equal tool to the gods' ears as rage and chaos. We will discover more about the practices used and the principle reasons behind calling the spirit realm.

From there we take a step into the world of runes and runestones and the power they wield. We will go over the characteristics of each rune language and its evolution over the 500 or so years, from the early Germanic migrations into the Medieval Period.

Rune magic cannot be explained without understanding the influence the gods had on each rune and the practice of casting them for divination, while also learning the methods and patterns applied to rune spreads and which rune to cast. The way in which you read the runes and the type of energy you put into the art is a practice that requires time and patience, allowing you to come back to this manuscript many times over.

Once we have finished that chapter, we can seep into the next section and enlighten you on the concept of Norse religion from birth to death—their enchanted connection to nature and wilderness along with the animals who roam it.

Lastly we will uncover the morals and ethics that upheld a civilization so strong, yet so malleable, allowing them to rule and be ruled.

On the arrival of the concluding chapter, we are sure that you will have a brighter and more integrated knowledge of Norse magic and the people who practiced it.

History Brought Alive is the leading author of historically significant books, this particular piece being no exception. So, without any further ado, enjoy!

Chapter 1: The Time & People

Norse culture is famously shrouded in mystery, where loose ends lay everywhere and the archeological world is beyond curious in finding the truth behind their daily and religious practices. There must be a distinct understanding of what it meant to be a Norseman and what other civilizations influenced and molded their culture. They existed as a group of people settling from their migrations as Germanic tribes up into the creeks and mountains of Scandinavia.

Let us take you back in time for a minute. The era is roughly between 500 and 800 C.E., called the Scandinavian Iron Age, and Roman influences are leaving a mark on these Scandinavian tribes that had migrated north from Germanic regions. The trading, warring, and interaction with these Romans passed on the beliefs and myths of their Roman pantheon onto the Northmen, thus evolving over the centuries into the Norse gods we know today.

Then, between 800 and 1100 C.E., the Viking Age was in full throttle. Ships were built, warriors were made, trades were finalized, and slaves were sold. The seas were the roads to new worlds, to riches, to new languages, and to a new god. Christian influence started taking hold both within Scandinavian kingdoms, introducing politics and economy, and within the many Viking settlements it also affected social and religious life.

The truth is that Norse history is a Sudoku puzzle. Bits and pieces try to fit into place in historians' minds, but it's almost impossible due to our obvious lack of context. That makes the incredible mystery even more intriguing as there is so much more to learn and discover each time!

More Than Just Norsemen

Norsemen is a term used for the Nordic people who lived in the North Atlantic region of what we know today as Scandinavia (Norway,

Denmark, Sweden, and later, Iceland). An Old Norse language was established based on Germanic and Indo-European origins before the Viking Age. Although basic agriculture collapsed by 550 C.E. and only restored towards the 8th century, historical evidence begins to show us a more detailed picture of set practices and beliefs coinciding with foreign influences. A more controlled paganism, if you will.

Their early society was not technically a literary one, and looking into their lives requires an understanding of their oral tradition, seen in early rune inscriptions and later in the sagas and poems. The stories were told, but the reasons and methods were left for interpretation.

The Norse were predominantly farmers, fishermen, and traders. It is often overlooked that their lifestyles were more than just pillaging and conquering. Their connection with their mythologies and their rituals of magic is rooted heavily in their actual day to day lives, rather than it being, for instance, a civilization polarized by different beliefs. They were unified and complex.

Daily Life

The Norsemen, as we call them today, were not connected to the name or function of Viking when at home in their Nordic countries. If you had to be in that time, Norse or Viking would not be a word you understood or conceptualized the way we do in the modern world. You were a part of a people who lived simply in the Scandinavian wilderness and who hunted, farmed, fished, cultivated livestock, spoke to the gods, and, at times, partook in civil war among neighboring villages and clans. Positions of hierarchy were established and overthrown many times, and slaves were commonplace. Kings and magnates (chieftains) were quite literally the men who owned the biggest farm or the most ships. Each clan or merchant town stood independent from the other and later, with social evolution, regions and kingdoms were formed.

A simple subsistence level of farm work and living in rural farmsteads was a picture of normal Norse life. Villages usually consisted of between 15 and 60 people depending on their location for trade and agriculture.

Throughout the Viking Age, social structures began to evolve and encompass three main tiers:

- The elite, who were the wealthiest families like kings or chieftains.
- The free men and women. Here we see the majority of the population who might have owned their own land, worked the farm, or traded goods and slaves.
- Slaves were known as thralls. Before slavery ended towards the late Middle Ages, the purchase and sale of human lives was considered standard practice.

Mortality rates were also very high and it is said that around 30–40% of children died before adulthood due to famine and diseases. We could see why the Vikings decided to venture to new lands, as theirs was hostile and unforgiving, especially in winter.

The trade routes of spices, silk, pottery, and silver were established and became a vital source of income as well as the trade of knowledge and information.

Curious by nature and strong by breeding, these people were tenacious and courageous, capable of feats that later civilizations would never reach. A mixture of magic and hard reality was what they lived and abided by—basic rules of engagement both with their peers and with the spirit world.

Slavery

Many historians turn to the belief that Viking raids were assembled first and foremost to enslave the local people and take them back to their country to make use of or trade with. Mainly women were captured, but men and children were also taken. The slave trade focused on the continent of Britain but also extended across the Mediterranean from Spain to Egypt.

The evidence seen besides oral accounts is in the finding of collars and shackles around the ancient urban centers. Slaves were used for many activities such as textile manufacturing, ship building, farming, and most of the unpleasant jobs done around the homestead. Sexual slavery as well as intermarriage was another reason the Vikings traded so loosely with the slave women and children of England and France.

Women

As the Norse had a very patriotic culture, most women stayed in the villages while the men went on their raids or fishing trips. Some women did join in sailing to other lands to settle with their families and some did really train as shield maidens and joined the men in battle. We speak of the free women who were wives, sisters, and daughters. Slave women were nowhere near treated the same.

The women had a strong standing when it came to matters of healing, magic and rituals. This book is centered on magic and ritualism, and women played a central part in that field.

Within the threshold of the home, women were in charge of preparing food, cleaning the house, purchasing and repairing clothing items, baking, cooking, preparing alcoholic drinks, and making dairy products. The men hunted and maintained their agriculture and livestock farming, though both women and men took the role of shepherd. In summer months, when the work was plenty, usually the whole household pulled their weight and assisted in the sowing and reaping.

Women did have a voice in gatherings and meetings, and were able to divorce their men if they chose. Such an oddity if you think how other civilizations operating at the time still held a very backwards view of marriage and fidelity. This is not to say that men were faithful in the way we know fidelity today.

Normally unions and weddings were arranged by the patriarch of the family, both for social uplifting and monetary gain, but seen too were relationships based on love and companionship.

More Than Just Vikings

Vikings were those who sailed the northern Atlantic seas to run raids or settle in new lands. The word Viking is technically the verb for "making a sea voyage" in the Old Norse language, so the Norsemen would "go Viking."

The period is now 800 C.E. and the Norsemen have mastered shipbuilding in a way that allowed them to navigate rough seas as well as narrow rivers with dexterity. The people are eager and strong, ready to venture to new lands. Many warriors were sailing across the Atlantic or traveling the Mediterranean, some strategizing river access to major cities across Europe, and others accessing the far regions of the East through the Baltic channels of trade. Other Norse-Icelandic people even attempted to settle in the Americas. The headgear they wore never consisted of horned helmets, as is usually portrayed in media, but rather simple iron helmets. This misrepresentation was established through Christian-influenced literature.

The pièce de résistance was their ability to sail. Building ships that were both agile and strong, they designed them with planks that followed the tree's grain, making them naturally stronger. The clinker method, which was a pattern for building the hull with overlapping planks riveted together, was ingenious in allowing flexibility with a comparatively lightweight and shallow depth structure. This allowed smooth navigation during raids where speed and maneuverability were crucial. With the addition of sun stones and sun charts that would track the sun's path over the sky during adverse weather, the Vikings were unstoppable.

Making use initially of water advantage, stealth, speed, and brute strength, the Vikings later evolved into a more sophisticated and political force and what some widely considered the reason the Viking Era ended.

Different Ventures

Historical resources from the first Viking raids in the late 7th century are terribly limited. What we do know is that the Norse were not strictly divided into separate states or regions as we may see now. The *Anar-Ulstar Chronicles* from Ireland and the *Anglo-Saxon Chronicles* mention that the Norwegians, Swedes, and Danish all considered themselves as different people and different groups. "The difference between these groups would have been small, if not imperceptible to our modern lens, but to the Vikings, they would have been paramount," (Adrien, 2021).

So it's safe to say that they were broadly separated into three main groups:

- The **Danish Vikings** were seen as the strongest of the factions, with a more militaristic people and a stronger political mind. They dominated over their initial raids and settlements and conquered with more ease. Due to their affinity for political agendas, they grew faster and stronger by ensuring their confirmation to Christianity would be conducive to gaining more title and protection over land and people.

Much more is known about the Danish Vikings than their cousins, and it is believed to mainly be due to the fact that they dominated regions that had people who were better at chronologizing and depicting the battles and events of history at the time.

They were able to both outwit and outmaneuver the enemy, which consisted mainly of Britain, Normandy (a region of France), and certain parts of the Mediterranean. The Danish settled well in Normandy where native women were taken as wives which brought about more social coercion.

- The **Swedish Vikings** were also known as Varangians or the Rus due to their founding the regions in what is known as Russia today. They were tradesmen and explorers, rather than pillagers and murderers like their counterparts. They excelled and focused their trade on the Middle Eastern areas of the Baltic. If you look at the map of Scandinavia, you will see that Sweden's waters face more eastwards than north or west, giving them more availability and access to those lands and regions. Being merchants and mercenaries too, the Swedes took to more honest work than raiding and pillaging. Being especially proud of their heritage, they were the last of the three groups to convert to Christianity.

- With the **Norwegian Vikings**, we see the most brave, crazed, and barbaric warriors of their time and standing. Berserkers (Vikings who wore the pelts of wolves and bears to bring strength in battle) were found among these warriors and were the only Vikings to be known to use the axe as a weapon in battle. The Norwegians were the best shipbuilders and sailors who reached the farthest coasts of Iceland, Greenland, and the Americas.

Icelandic Settlements

During the 9th century, Iceland was covered in forests and woodlands, and was quite a bit warmer than the Scandinavian lands to the east. Both unsettled and rich in resources, it was perfect for the taking, allowing them to settle there for around 56 years.

The Norwegians were the first to sail to Iceland, with the settlement of Ingólfr Arnarson broadly being considered the first settler in 874 C.E. Thanks to the ample details given in the *Landnámabók* writings of the 13th century, we can find more historical information about Norse life in the Icelandic sagas and stories than anywhere else.

The genetic makeup of human remains in these lands suggests that many of the settlers were of Irish and Scottish descent, with a smaller portion hailing from Scandinavia. This meant that there must have been a great intermingling of cultures during the settlement age. We know that the settlement failed and many of the initial settlers either died due to harsh conditions or returned home.

Conflicts and Raids

Along with the constant civil conflicts between Scandinavian kingdoms, which were led by kings and earls to gain land and power, the conflicts occurring overseas and in Europe were far more organized and strategic. Even though many of the raids were on English monasteries, this was not due to their hatred of the religion, but for the easy access and weakly defended wealth in these locations.

The raiding of monasteries was already in play by late 700 C.E. in England, and now it was time to take advantage of the resources available and begin a prosperous trade, both in goods and in slaves. In the Viking's eyes, this is no terrible thing. It is a concept of the strong taking from the weak, not the wicked taking from the good.

Their Influence

The one thing that still allows us to study and evaluate their ancient lives is what they left behind for us—all those relics that have survived so long. But one influence that remains close to many hearts is their social influence on various other cultures at the time, like the Celts and the Gaels.

The Celts

During the Bronze Age, the Celts and Vikings were the largest groups to inhabit the northern world, and the fusion between the two was inevitable. The Celts inhabited northern England, Scotland, and Ireland but also spread to Northern Italy and Spain. Some think that due to similarity in language and culture there is a genetic connection between Vikings and Celts. The truth of the matter is that they were equally influenced by each other but had no genetic correlation. Celtic people were not seafarers and were more oriented in growing their own lands than pillaging others.

The Celts and ancient Germanic people were neighbors before they decided to migrate and settle in separate lands during the Dark Ages. The Celts took to Ireland and Scotland from their Indo-European and Anatolian migration while the Germanic people mostly settled in Scandinavia.

During the Viking Age, the Celts had more influence on the Vikings in culture and language as they were already Christianized by the 5th century, whereas the Vikings contributed riches and the contact with foreign goods from trades.

The Vikings landed in Ireland around the 7th century after having had some practice raiding and pillaging in East England and Scotland. They were incredibly important in the foundation of some major Irish towns known today, like Dublin and Cork. This clearly tells us that there was not solely violence, but some diplomacy and shared trade too.

Ancient Celtic tribes did not invent their own runic language; it was adopted from the Norse influence before and during the migrations, where both feuds and social interactions took place.

The Norse-Gaels

These people were a mix of Norsemen and people from Ireland, called the Gaelic. When the Viking Age was in full bloom around the 9th century, the settlers that arrived in Ireland and Scotland interbred with the local people, adopting language and customs. Leaving behind the Norse gods and converting to Christianity was termed Gaelicization. This meant that their culture was altered to such a degree in influence over a few generations that they considered themselves more Gaelic than Norse.

Even after the conversion and after the Norse-Gaels disappeared entirely as a people, they still left a long lasting history in Ireland and Scotland. For instance, many Irish towns bear Norse-Gaelic names and the Scottish gallowglass warmongers were descendants of these people.

Chapter 2: The Gods & Realms

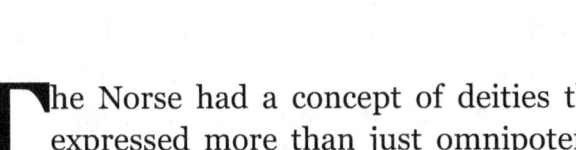

The Norse had a concept of deities that expressed more than just omnipotence and fear, but also knowledge and kindness. These gods inspire countless myths and folktales around creation and destruction. Each having a specific character reference and theme, they were more than ethereal powers in another reality, but real flesh and blood beings that directly affected their everyday lives.

As we take you further into the book and touch more on the subjects of influence from Christian ideas, you will notice that the inscriptions of historical myths change depending on the time written. The various gods were depicted differently depending on who wrote it, sometimes adding or removing certain characteristics of their theme and influence. The alteration is best seen in the aspects and powers of the female deities' beings transferring into that of male deities, centralizing the worship in patriarchal figures. Even more, the various names given to the gods and realms are sometimes changed or altered with a literature largely more descriptive and narrative than its earlier works.

The information between pre-Christian influences and post-Christian influences on historical events has a major impact on accuracy and truth. What we mainly know of their stories comes through late 19th century poems and sagas from Icelandic mythographer Snorri Sturluson, who was already a Christian at the time and wrote with that mentality, thus changing the themes accordingly to his views.

The Pantheon

The most powerful magic known to the gods was that of seiðr, the power to see fates, and it was first and foremost practiced by the goddess Freyja of the Vanir. Due to equal jealousy, disapproval, and fear of this power, another group of gods called the Æsir, who were more prone to the use of weapons and brute strength rather than magic, waged wars on the Vanir. As was customary, wagers were eventually met to stop the fighting, and hostages from each group were given to the other as a peace treaty. Therefore as seen below, the pantheon certainly does contain more Æsir gods than their Vanir counterparts, but their intermingling in mythology helps create more intricate stories and themes.

The Æsir became the more prominently known gods associated with war and strength, while the Vanir were more associated with fertility, magic, and agriculture. The Æsir reside in the realm of Asgard and the Vanir in lands of Vanaheim.

The Æsir

- Odin

    Known as the All-father, god of war, king of Asgard, bearer of wisdom and searcher of truth, Odin forms the head in the Triad of the mightiest gods, next to Thor and Freyja. Considered the first *sieðmann* (or male seer), he is known for his fervent pursuit of knowledge and is both revered for his standing in the pantheon as war leader and also shamed for his practice of seiðr magic, which was seen as a weakness in the use of it by men. Both Odin and the goddess Freyja are heavily associated with shamanism and the use of seiðr magic.

Odin is mainly worshiped in the pursuit of nobility, wealth, and prestige. He is acknowledged in helping mankind but also instigating and creating war for his own fickle purposes of gaining the most valuable warriors in his hall of Valhalla. It is said that he also has a general disregard for fairness and the law, making him more of a ruler by chaos rather than by peace. His use of magic and cunning to control is what makes him both deviant and inspiring.

He is the son of Borr and Bestla, along with his brothers Vili and Vé, arriving upon the creation of the universe. He is associated with his eight-legged horse Sleipnir, with whom he rides into battle and visits the underworld within countless stories. The two wolves, Geri and Freki, are usually by his side; and most noticeably, the two black ravens, Huginn and Muninn, are the projections of Odin and bring him information from Midgard, the realm of men. In his possession is always the spear Gungnir, which is often used in self-injury to sacrifice himself for the knowledge of all things, and the gold ring, Draupnir.

He is married to Freyja, the goddess of motherhood and love, often interchanged with the goddess Frigg in some tales. They have three sons: Baldr, Hermod, and Hodor. He is also famously the father or Thor, whose mother is the earth goddess, Jörð. The day of the week associated with Odin is Wednesday due to his other Old English name Woden.

- Thor

    The god of thunder, often seen as the hero of the common man, was the most worshiped god during the pre-Christian Scandinavian Era. He is associated with strength, the protection of mankind, and storms. The characteristics most valuable to the Norse people often surrounded Thor, like honor, loyalty, and the unshakable sense of duty. It was also his place to bless and consecrate holy places with his hammer Mjölnir, but in the same light it could also be used for destruction. A dual purpose of the mighty hammer reflects the dual properties of human existence. During the Christianization of Scandinavia, the image of Mjölnir was a tool for private revolt against the new God. Wearing pendants in the shape of the hammer was a deliberate contrast to the symbol of the cross.

Thor seems to fall onto the second tier in the deity scheme, which is the function of warrior and military power. Being the god of both tempestuous storms and sunny, fair weather, he is married to Sif, a golden-haired goddess linked to the earth and crops. Their marriage is often considered the divine marriage of sky and land.

His familiars are the two goats, Tanngrisnir and Tanngnjóstr, who pull his chariot, and of course his famous hammer Mjölnir. The day of the week dedicated to him is Thursday, from the Old Norse term *thorsdagr* meaning "Thor's day."

- Loki

    The sometimes malicious and sometimes helpful god of mischief is known to be part jötun (giant) and part deity. He holds a very unique position within the pantheon and contradicts the many notions Odin and Thor stand for. He "is portrayed as a scheming coward who cares only for the shallow pleasures of self-preservation" (McCoy, 2009), often using his shapeshifting abilities for that very purpose.

Loki is son to the giant, Fárbauti, and the goddess, Laufey. With his wife Sigyn, he sired the god Nif, and with the giantess Angreboða he sired the wolf, Fenrir, the giant serpent, Jörmungandr, and the goddess of the underworld, Hel.

His name is often thought to derive from the most direct translation of 'knot' or 'tangle,' which may very well be his main influence on the events in the mythologies. He holds a theme of contradicting the nature of things by shapeshifting and disguising himself often in female forms to deceive or to trick. He's not necessarily seen as a god like his counterparts, as no trace of worship for this deity has been found.

- Baldr

This particular god has a central, positive role in mythology due to his overall good nature and cheerful demeanor. Scholars disputed what function he might hold in the mythology, but he is often associated with love, peace, and forgiveness.

His benevolent, handsome, and gracious themes were more heavily constructed at the end of the Viking Age, when poets and skalds (poets who write skaldic poetry) were creating literature through a Christian lens. This can be seen in the idea of him shining like the sun, and having died and been resurrected, thus removing the original warlike disposition of the god from original pagan sources.

Baldr is the son of Odin and Frigg and is married to Nanna. He is the father of the god Foresti. Nanna and Foresti are obscure and are rarely mentioned in earlier works.

- Heimdallr

  Known as the god of foresight, guardian of the Bifröst Bridge, and watcher over Asgard, he resides in his high fortress called Himinbjörd and is depicted to have brilliant eyesight and hearing so he may watch with diligence over the worlds. He possesses the horn of Gjallarhorn to alert Asgardians of intruders. Some agree that he is the son of nine mothers, who are the nine daughters of the giant Aegir.

The other gods who are part of the Æsir are:

- Odin's two brothers, Vili and Vé, who together form the Triad of Spirit, Will, and Holiness.
- Hœnir, who assisted Odin in the creation of man.
- Týr, the one-handed god associated with the rules of law and heroic glory.
- Máni and Sól, the representation of the moon and sun.
- Bragi, the bard of Valhalla, responsible for welcoming the fallen warriors into the hall, and his wife Idun who cares for the fruit tree in Asgard that gives everlasting life.

The Vanir

- Freyja

This is the most powerful goddess in Asgard. She is associated with love, sexuality, fertility, seiðr, beauty, and death. She is an honorary member of the Æsir like her father and brother. Norse women worshiped her for their feminine needs and practices, especially in family protection and health.

She is most commonly portrayed as the goddess personification of the völva who practices seiðr magic. Sometimes depicted as promiscuous and unfaithful to her husband, the goddess often manipulates those around her according to her will. Ruling over her field of Fólkvangr, she receives half the warriors who die in battle for her hall, thus she is strongly connected to both war practices and the ideal of shamanism and magic.

Important to note is that in many accounts she and the goddess Frigg are often one and the same, as Frigg is married to Oðr, which translates to Odin. The post-Christian Germanic split went underway around the 10th century. Meaning we can easily assume the assimilation of the two goddesses becoming one at some point in history.

Freyja derives from the Old Norse word 'lady' which can be perceived more as a title than a name.

Freyja is the daughter of god Njorðr and sister to the god Freyr. She is married to Odin and has two daughters, Hnoss and Gersemi, along with her three sons. Her familiars consist of her chariot pulled by two male cats, which were gifts from Odin. She also owns the boar Hildisvíni and wears a cloak of falcon feathers that allows her to shapeshift into the bird. The day of the week mentioned to Freyja/Frigg is Friday, attested as *frigdæag* meaning "Frigg's day."

- Freyr

This god is connected to fair weather, sunshine, virility, and sacral kingship. He is known as the god that bestows peace and pleasure to the mortals. He is often worshiped at weddings and harvest festivals for his themes of both sexual and ecological fertility. Boars were sacrificed to Freyr at weddings, especially the boar Gullinbursti as his familiar, and this was the main symbolism of his virility.

He is the son of the god Njorðr and brother to the goddess Freyja. He presides over the realm of Alfheim, which was given to him as a teething present, and later marries the giantess Gerðr. His familiars are his boar Gullinbursti and his magical sword Sumarbrander, which could fight on its own. He also sails the ship Skiðblanðir, which always sees good weather and which could be magically folded away into a carry bag.

The god is known to be a lover to many goddesses, giantesses, and even his own sister Freyja, as incest was not frowned upon by the Vanir. His name, like that of his sister Freyja (lady), means 'lord.'

- Njorðr

Like his children, Freyja and Freyr, Njorðr is a representative of fertility. He also encompasses the ideologies of wealth and, most noticeably, he is considered the god of seas and seafaring where he resides in his beach kingdom, Nóatún.

He is the principle god of the Vanir and, unfortunately, very little is known about him as he was mostly worshiped during the initial stages of the Viking Era, therefore giving us few resources to work with.

The Valkyries

What we know of the Valkyries today, being graceful shield maidens who fly to battle with their lord Odin and retrieve the souls of fallen warriors to take to Odin's hall, might be another Christianization and softening of their actual roles from original pagan times. It is found that their original traits were far more insidious—they personify the carnage of war and at some points are depicted as wearing intestines as belts and using heads as weights.

It was thought that the goddess Freyja was the leader of the Valkyries, as she would retrieve for herself half of the fallen warriors for her fields in Fólkvangr, while the other souls would either be taken to Valhalla by the Valkyries or go to the realm of the Underworld, Hel (which is where most common folk were thought to go).

There is knowledge of many Valkyries, but six in particular are mentioned in the Eddas:

- Skuld (debt)
- Skogul (shaker)
- Gunnr (war)
- Hildr (battle)
- Gondul (wand-wielder)
- Geirskogul (spear-bearer)

Cosmology

There are nine realms existing in Norse cosmology. The center of their universe and what connects all the realms together is situated in Asgard, and it is known as Yggdrasil, the World Tree.

The story from the *Völuspá* poem describes the events that took place during the creation of all things.

Two great realms once existed: one of ice and one of fire. They were separated by a terrible void called the Ginnungagap. These realms were to be known as Niflheim and Muspelheim, in turn. From the eventual collision of these realms, the ice on Niflheim melted and revealed

Ymir, the proto-giant, and a cow called Audhumla.

Now, Audhumla licked away at the ice and uncovered Búri, forefather of the gods. Audhumla and Búri sired son Borr and daughter Bestla, who in turn sired the brother gods known as Odin, Vili, and Vé. The three brothers take it upon themselves to kill Ymir so that they may create the world of men from his remains. Flesh for earth, skull for sky, bones for mountains, and blood for sea. The World Tree emerged soon after the world's creation along with all the many beings and realms. Once it was all done, with the help of god Baldr, from the deep woods emerged the first two humans, named Ask and Embla, and they began populating the new realm.

The early Norse works of Eddic and Skaldic poetry assumes the reader has knowledge of the cosmology, and thus, not much explanation is given on location and specific characteristics. Although Snorri's work of the nine realms changed it slightly adding and removing realms to include Helheim, or Hel (the Underworld), there is an importance of understanding that in Scandinavia at the time these descriptions would probably not be recognized and be quite different. Theirs was a living dynamic faith, and our knowledge is but just the surface of a much larger iceberg.

Nine Realms

Their mythology had various details about the worlds created and some written sources are less clear than the others. What were known to be the original nine realms are

- Godheim - Realm of Æsir (Asgard)
- Alfheim - Realm of Bright Elves
- Svartalfheim - Realm of Black Elves
- Niflheim - Realm of Ice and Mist
- Muspelheim - Realm of Fire and Chaos
- Mannheim - Realm of Men and Trolls (Midgard)
- Jötunheim - Realm of Giants (Utgard)
- Nidavelir - Realm of the Dwarves
- Vanaheim - Realm of the Vanir

Yggdrasil and the Norns

An ash I know there stands, Yggdrasil is its name, a tall tree, showered with shining loam. From there come the dews that drop on the

> *valleys, it stands forever green over Uror's well.*
>
> —*Völuspá in the Poetic Edda.*

Yggdrasil, the World Tree, is thought to be the center of the Norse universe. The origins of the name have various sources, but it is generally understood as 'gallows' in Old Norse.

Situated in the realm of Asgard, upon its roots live multiple creatures and beings: the dragon of death, Níðhöggr, the four stags Dáinn, Duneyrr, Dvalinn, and Duraþrór who eat at the branches and roots, and the great unnamed eagle. Below the roots lies the Serpent of the World that chokes the roots surrounding Midgard. The tree has three roots that feed on three different wells: the Well of Urd in Asgard, the Well of Mímir by the frost giants, and the Hvergelmir Well in Niflheim.

But most importantly we see the connection to the three Norns: Uror, Verðandi, and Skuld. Their purpose is to nourish the World Tree with water from the sacred Well of Urd to prevent it from dying, and to twine the threads of fates of all things, often thought to be the roots of the tree themselves. They are secretive and unseen, rarely revealing their fateful secrets to men.

They could be malevolent or benevolent, often determining the future of newborn children.

Ragnarök

Ragnarök was known to all. It was the inevitable end of all things both divine and mortal. The concept that war and destruction would take hold of the realms through fire was what every commoner, slave, and king believed. Therefore, one could say that their fate was set in stone.

Initially attested in the Poetic Edda in the 13th century by Snorri Sturlersun, it was written as the *Twilight of the Gods*. What we see is a long and interesting poem told by the völva, who visits a village and prophesies the end of all things. She tells us of the clash between the gods and giants, the deceit of some, and the loss of loved ones due to others. The fire giants burn the worlds and all that is left is a few gods and a few humans who step out of the destruction to begin the world anew. It is important to the Norse that a theme of renewal comes through the final chapter, as nothing is ever the end.

Trolls, Dwarves, Elves, and

Giants

Trolls

Some tales from Sweden describe trolls as monstrous beings with many heads who can either live in the forest and mountains or in caves. The first kind of trolls that live in the mountains are known to be large, aggressive, stupid, and slow beings, always getting outwitted by the hero in the story. Those that live in caves are shy and seen as shorter than humans with stumpy arms and legs but with a fair amount of intelligence. They use the environment around them to influence their power or protect themselves and hide. These creatures emerged into mythology from the idea of the giants (jötun) in their cosmology and realms, as the word troll in Old Norse is *jätte*.

Dwarves

The dwarves were known to be crafty beings that live in the realm of Midgard, hidden from humans in subterranean realms. The tales of dwarves go far back into mythology and creation, as they were known to be born of the flesh of the giant Ymir, along with the rest of their cosmos. They were molded by the Æsir into figures that resemble humans, but much shorter and gifted with intelligence and skill. These beings are artists in creating all sorts of things from jewelry to weapons and other intricate pieces. We see their skill in the creation of Thor's hammer Mjölnir crafted by the dwarves Brokkr and Eitri, as well as many other weapons in the gods' possession.

Elves

The elves, as from the many references we have in popular culture today, are known to be fair, beautiful, and tall beings that are swift in battle and powerful with magic. Initially, in pre-Christian myths, these demi-gods were one class of being who lived in one realm. Later, their mythology developed and they were divided into Light Elves (Ljösáfar) that lived in the realm of Alfheim reigned by the god Freyr, and the Dark Elves (Dökkálfar) that lived deep within the earth and had a darker complexion. Elves were known to cause illness to the humans and, when offered something in return, they could heal them too. Humans were known to also become elves after they died due to the connection of the worship of ancestors to the worship of elves.

Giants

These supernatural beings of the natural world have, from the beginning of time, been the arch rivals of the Æsir and Vanir. They often warred, fought, cheated, and married each other. The *jötun* live in the icy realm of Jötunheim, which is closely connected to Midgard by mountain ranges and dense forests, while the fire giants live in Múspellsheimr, their realm of fire. They are the catalyst of the great ending in Ragnarök, setting fire to the tree Yggdrasil and ending everything in flame.

What one would think of giants in physique is their immense stature, but in fact they were no bigger than an average human and resembled the humanoid beings of other realms. They represented the original nature of chaos and destruction in comparison to the gods representing life and order.

Chapter 3: The Myth & Folklore

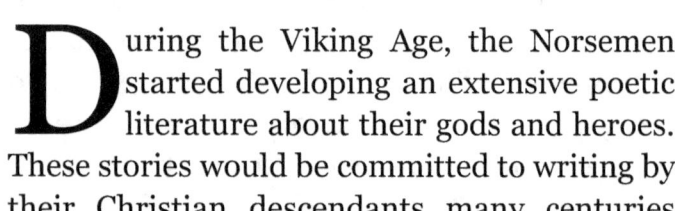

During the Viking Age, the Norsemen started developing an extensive poetic literature about their gods and heroes. These stories would be committed to writing by their Christian descendants many centuries later.

The characters within these poems often act in a way that is incompatible with the social norms that we are accustomed to in our present day. The warlike and aggressive attitude in men and in the gods they worshiped has been associated with their lack of resources and harsh climate in Medieval Scandinavia. Fighting for these resources and the aggression against their neighbors was not necessarily considered wrong or unjust. If it advanced their wealth and honor, then it was only fair for them to take what is deserved. The honor gained and maintained by confronting enemies with strength and valor was a moral in itself. A readiness to use violence in return for violence done to one's friends and relatives was commonplace and reflected in the characters of many of the gods that, in our society today, would probably be considered barbaric and cruel.

It must be stated that a person's word was considered absolutely binding and stood stronger than the family unit or even the self. Many of the stories shadow the choice the hero has to make to either keep his word by then having to hurt or kill the people closest to him or lose his honor by choosing the loved ones life over the oath made.

The stories and poems are attuned to the strict class structure present at the time, most noticeably in the Poetic Edda. The characters are tightly bound to these social structures and don't deviate from them. If one was of noble birth, then they would not consider the life of the common free man any more than they would a dog roaming the village. Large differences in activities, dress, and diet expected of people at different social levels were the stepping stone to the rest of the story.

> "Heed my words all classes of men, you greater and lesser children of Heimdall."
>
> –*Völuspá in Poetic Edda*

Another noteworthy characteristic of Norse poems is the idea that all people had predetermined and fixed dates of death determined by the Norns who sit at their pool and weave their fates. "A man would not live one day longer than the Norns had decided. The characters in these myths are marching towards their doom, unable to change course or step off their predetermined path even if they fight it the entire way" (Crawford, 2021).

The boldness and defiance of their fates must have galvanized something in the Norse audience surrounded by their cold rural farmsteads. Many of the stories end in tragedy, but that need not mean they left the audience in despair; it was simply the light and dark realities of life.

Mythologies and legends living within Norse culture are either minimal in their true pre-Christian pagan times, or are post-Christian and influenced by Latin poets and writers. Scandinavian cultures were an overwhelmingly oral society in the retelling of history. Many holes and loose threads are present in the current knowledge of their customs. "Although some of these tell complete myths, most of them assume - unfortunately for us - that their audience was familiar with the mythical context" (Groenavelde, 2017).

The Eddas

The Eddas are a collection of two Medieval Icelandic manuscripts of mythology that use prose (stories) and poems in different stanzas to describe, depict, and detail the religion, cosmology, and history of ancient Scandinavian culture. The composition of the poems can either use the Eddaic or Skaldic genre of poetry and mainly uses alliterative versing and symbolism.

It is still unsure where the term 'Edda' derives from exactly, and there are quite a few hypotheses, but the easiest etymology to point towards is the Old Norse word *óðr* meaning 'poetry.'

The two collections of work are known as the Poetic Edda and the Prose Edda.

Poetic Edda

Poetic Edda, or Elder Edda, is a compilation of Icelandic and Norwegian tales that first appeared in the 13th century and is contained in the *Codex Regius* or "Royal Book." Many other poems were added to the Poetic Edda over the years and they were composed with visionary force and dramatic quality.

The Poetic Edda was more often written in an Eddic genre of poetry and follows these four rules:

- The author is anonymous.
- It uses a certain meterage (*fornyröislag*, *ljóðaháttr*, and *málaháttr*).
- It has a direct approach to word order.
- Kennings (ancient figures of speech) are used less.

By far the most extensive source of Norse mythology, the Poetic Edda consists of two separate parts: the Mythological Poems and the Heroic Lays.

The Mythological Poems tell us about the adventures of the gods from their own perspectives and carries eleven poems: Völuspá, Hávamál, Vafþrúðnismál,

Grimnismál, Skirnismál, Hábarðsljóð, Hymiskviða, Lokasenna, Þrymskviða, Völundarkviða, and Alvíssmál.

The Heroic Lays, in three parts, depicts the challenges and journeys of heroes and heroines and carries nineteen songs:

- The Helgi Lays consisting of six stories:

Helgakviða Hundingsbana I, Helgakviða Hjörvarðssonar, Helgakviða Hundingsbana II, Helgakviða Hundingsbana I, Helgakviða Hjörvarðssonar, and *Helgakviða Hundingsbana II.*

- The Niflung Cycle consisting of fifteen stories:

Frá dauða Sinfjötla, Grípisspá, Reginsmál, Fáfnismál, Sigrdrífumál, Brot af Sigurðarkviðu, Guðrúnarkviða I, Sigurðarkviða hin skamma, Heimreið Brynhildar, Dráp Niflunga, Guðrúnarkviða II, Guðrúnarkviða III, Oddrúnargrátr, Atlakviða, and *Atlamál hin grenienzku.*

- The Jörmunrekkr Lays consisting of two stories:

Guðrúnarhvöt, Hamðismál.

Prose Edda

Prose Edda, or Younger Edda, is an Icelandic textbook written in the 13th century. Scholars assume that a large part of the text was written by law speaker and poet Snorri Sturluson. He was known for a verse use that was reflective of court poetry, putting him in higher esteem with peers.

> Snorri Sturluson has long proven a paradoxical figure for those who think and write about medieval Norse culture. Many scholars believe that a satisfactory understanding of Snorri and his work will only be possible once the contradictions that surround this most famous medieval Icelander have been resolved. (Wanner, 2008)

The recomposing of stories altered the characteristics and influences of the gods in some writings but made them easier to comprehend.

The Prose Edda was typically written in the skaldic genre of poetry following these rules:

- The author is known.

- Ornate meterage is used (*dróttkvætt* or a variation).
- Sentences are commonly interwoven and contain ornate syntax.
- Kennings are often used.

The Prose Edda consists of four sections:

- Prologue
- Gylfaginning
- Skáldskaparmál
- Háttatal

The Icelandic Sagas

Staying around the 12th to 13th century, we see a composition written in Old Icelandic of accounts in prose format, meaning that the story is written in a narrative progression rather than the more poetically composed Elder Eddas. They depicted the events that occurred in the 9th and 10th century settlement stage. The term 'saga' derives from Old Norse and translates as 'utterance' or "oral account."

During the settlement of Iceland, also known as the Saga Age, most accounts were pre-Christian and their authentic and detailed retellings of their pagan world are what make them so precious and valuable. These family sagas are especially complete in their family connections and detailed genealogy. There are stories of struggle and conflict, and they give us a broader picture of their culture and practices.

These sagas can then further be separated into the King's sagas (sagas of legendary Nordic kings), Legendary sagas (Norse sagas accounting pre-Icelandic settlement), and the Contemporary sagas (mainly the accounts of the Sturlunga family).

The un-surety of authorship from these pieces of work allow for more study and discussion, but many like to attribute some to Snorri Sturluson, in the case of Egil's Saga.

Some Stories and Themes

The relation to love and lust and the surrounding principle of marriage are central to many stories in Norse mythology. The hero either has to win his affection or cheat for such affection, always simplifying the exception of the female characters in some way by giving in or being the weaker sex that should not fight back.

Another is the relation to destiny and fate. The Norns are seen as some of the most important and strong beings in the Norse universe. They control all the fates woven through Yggdrasil and weave them according to divine plans. Even though Odin does receive the knowledge of the runes, they were still only given to him and never really his. Therefore, one can say that the mythological stories centered on the pursuit and inevitable connections to one's own fate are highly regarded.

Another strong theme in the tales and myths is revenge. It was a common idea that one could take the hurt they felt for either being deceived or angered by another and return that pain tenfold. The vengeful characters and gods who were too proud or vain to be deceived would plan and strategize this theme, even if it meant their mutual destruction.

Skirnismál: The Lay of Skírnir (Poetic Edda)

The god Freyr sits on Odin's throne, *Hliðskjálf,* and looks out over the many worlds. As his eyes pass over the realm of giants,

Jötunheimr, he sees a beautiful giantess named Gerðr and is taken by desire to pursue her.

Freyr cannot bring himself to speak with her directly, fearing doom and rejection, but the goddess Skaði, wife of Njördr, sees his gloom and asks if Freyr's servant Skírnir could inquire about the sulking god.

Skírnir is told by Freyr that he is afraid and unable to speak to her, and he asks if maybe Skírnir could go talk to her in his stead. Of course Skírnir agrees and is given Freyr's faithful steed and his magical sword to go forth and woo this giantess on his behalf.

Once he arrives in Jötunheimr and steps into the hall of giants, the beautiful Gerðr sees him and greets him kindly. Skírnir, not one to waste time, jumps straight into the songs to express the desire his master, Freyr, has for the giantess. His many attempts to get her to accept a meeting with Freyr are shut down, even after bribing with gifts and chanting melodies of lust. Frustrated and most likely tired, Skírnir resorts to some forceful and violent threats towards her and her father if she doesn't agree to the rendezvous:

> "Seest thou, maiden, this keen bright sword

> That I hold here in my hand?
>
> Before its blade the old giant bends,—
>
> Thy father is doomed to die.
>
> I strike thee, maid, with my gambantein
>
> To tame thee to work my will;
>
> There shalt thou go where never again
>
> The sons of men shall see thee" (p. 115).

So now Skírnir has threatened enough and Gerðr accepts the request for a meeting with this god. Content with having done his duty, Skírnir returns to Freyr in Asgard and before he can get off the horse and hand back the sword, Freyr is there to quickly know how it went:

> Tell me, Skírnir, before unsaddling
>
> Or stepping forth another pace
>
> Is the news you bring from Jötunheim
>
> For better or for worse? (p. 119)

Skírnir replies:

> In the woods of Barri, which know we both so well,

> A quiet still and tranquil place
>
> In nine night time to Njörd's son
>
> Will Ger-ðr give herself. (p. 120)

How delightful and excited Freyr is! He responds:

> One night is long enough, yet longer still are two;
>
> How then shall I contend with three?
>
> For months have passed more quickly
>
> Than half a bridal eve. (p. 120)

The idea of the curses laid out gives significance to what power and masculinity the Æsir hold over the females of other worlds. The concept of romanticism and lust hold strong meaning in many tales.

This could have possibly translated to the patriarchic and forceful nature of men at the time towards unclaimed women, meaning that the choice was there, but if chosen incorrectly, then either death or shame would come your way.

Frithiof's Saga (Legendary Saga by Esaias Tegnér)

King Beli of Sogn had two sons, Helgi and Halfdan, and a beautiful prized daughter named Ingeborg. Now King Beli had many friends, but his closest friend was his neighbor Thorstein, who lived across the fjord. Thorstein's own son, Frithiof, was a strong and bold man, known for his bravery and physical height.

Ingeborg's mother unfortunately passed away when they were young, and one of King Beli's goodmen, Hilding, took Ingeborg and her brothers, as well as young, strapping Frithiof under his wing as foster-father, so all the children had grown up together and become fast friends. Over the years, Frithiof found a deep and maddening love for Ingeborg that bloomed from childhood into their adult lives.

During a civil war, both King Beli and Frithiof's father, Thorstein, were killed on the battlefield, leaving the two brothers, Helgi and Halfdan, as brother-kings to rule over the kingdom. The brothers were particularly jealous of Frithiof and his incredible qualities of bravery and strength and were aware of his desire for their sister. In a petty and sly maneuver, the brothers transferred Ingeborg to a sacred dwelling far away called Baldrshagi, where intercourse and love relations were forbidden. This never deterred Frithiof's devotion to Ingeborg and still he visited her and they continued to share their love.

This angered the brother-kings terribly, so they took action and sent Frithiof off to the Orkney Islands in Scotland in an excuse to put distance between him and their fair sister. While away to pay tribute as requested, the brothers decide to burn down Frithiof's house and marry Ingeborg off to the Norwegian King Ring of Ringerike. Surely Ingeborg is mortified and obeys nonetheless, but her beloved Frithiof has no idea what has transpired.

Upon his return to Norway and finding the remains of his homestead and the absence of his love Ingeborg, he inquired with the brother-kings and discovered their treachery. In a rage, he burned down the sacred temple of Baldrshagi where Ingeborg once stayed, and took up his weapon and shield to sail to far lands as a Viking.

For three years he ventured, raided, and traded, gaining many riches and a grand reputation. When he returns home he decides to take up winter residence with King Ring so he may be closer to Ingeborg once more. Frithiof is a noble and kind man, so naturally he becomes strong friends with the old king. Just before the king's death, Frithiof is named earl of King Ring's domain and care-taker of Ingeborg's first child. He then marries Ingeborg almost immediately, finally getting the love he craved all his life.

After the death of the old king, Frithiof takes up his revenge against the petty and untrustworthy brothers who he grew up with. He kills the eldest brother and makes the youngest a liege of his kingdom, bound to his service. And so the patient and valiant Frithiof now can rest and love in peace.

This inspiring and immortal Scandinavian tale of love, conquest, and revenge has many variations, but the moral is always the same. Ture love does not need to be rushed. Patience, courage, and honor will guide the true hearted on their path to happiness.

Grímnismál: The Lay of Grímnir (Poetic Edda)

King Hraudung had two sons: Agnar, the oldest, was ten winters old, and his younger brother Geirröd was eight. They both enjoyed fishing together and decided to row the boat out so they may catch some small fish. Being preoccupied by the task at hand, they had not noticed how far the wind had driven them out into the open sea. Stranded till dark, they were eventually wrecked onto shore out in the country.

Cold, hungry, and tired, they walked up to the nearest cottage they could find, where a peasant and his wife lived. They welcomed the boys into their home and kept them for the winter, where they taught the two boys many things and gave them sound advice. The wife took charge of the younger Agnar, and the husband mentored Geirröd.

Once spring had come along, the husband and wife assisted the brothers in returning to their kingdom with a ship they procured. Accompanying them along the journey back home, they had good weather and spoke about many things.

Once the ship arrived at shore, Geirröd jumped off the ship with speed and pushed the ship back out to sea with force while insulting the two peasants as they drifted away. Geirröd managed to return home and the people were rejoiced, but his father, the king, had died, therefore it was Geirröd's time to be king. He and his kingdom prospered. On the other hand, his younger brother Agnar went to live in a cave with a giantess.

Now Odin is sitting on his throne, Hlidskjalf, with his wife Frigg beside him, watching over the worlds in quiet contemplation. As they gaze over Midgard, the realm of men, Odin notices how his foster-son Geirröd was going for himself as king, while Agnar, Frigg's foster-son, was simply living in a cave with his giantess.

Odin and Frigg often enjoyed disguising themselves as humans, and they were the two peasants who had helped the stranded brothers that winter many moons ago.

Frigg, offended, responded by saying that King Geirröd was very frugal and inhospitable if he knew that too many guests would consume his food stores and other resources.

The two gods argued over this until they decided to settle it with wager. Frigg would send her maid Fulla to the king, where Fulla would inform him that soon one night an evil magician would come calling at his court and that this magician could be recognized by the fact that the hounds would not show aggression towards him. So, Fulla does her goddesses bidding and King Geirröd heeds the advice given.

Not long after, Odin, in disguise, does appear in a dark blue cloak at the king's home, and just like the maiden had advised, the hounds were tame towards the man. This man was immediately imprisoned and would only say that he was named Grímnir, and no more.

King Geirröd tortured Grímnir for more information by placing him between two fires for eight nights. In pity, Agnar, the king's young son named after his uncle, decides to help the man and offers him a drink, complaining that his father did not have to be so cruel. Grímnir tells Agnar that no one else had bothered to assist him during these horrendous eight days and nights of torture, and upon burning his cloak in the fire he reveals himself as the All-father. Odin had prophesied that Agnar would become Lord of the Goths and promised him great reward for his kindness.

Fire! thou art hot,

and much too great;

flame! let us separate.

My garment is singed,

although I left it up,

my cloak is scorched before it.

...

Eight night have I sat

between fires here,

food has offered,

save only Agnar,

the son of Geirröd,

who alone shall rule

over the land of the Goths.

...

Be thou blessed, Agnar!

as blessed as the god of men

bids thee to be.

For one draught

> thou never shalt
>
> get better recompense. (p. 20)

Odin then teaches Agnar about the expanse of the known cosmology and many realms that exist and all the beings that live there, and tells him the names of his many other disguises.

Odin reveals himself to the king as well and promises him misfortune for the treatment he has received. King Geirröd, understanding the severity of the mistake made, attempts to retrieve the man from the fires but in doing so his sword, which was lying on his lap, slips and falls hilt down. In a rush, the king stumbles and falls upon the open blade where he immediately dies. Odin disappears in that moment, and Agnar becomes the new king who rules from that day forth with more generosity and kindness.

Please note that only the first three of the 54 stanzas of Odin's monologue were inserted into the above depiction of the tale, as maybe the full 54 would be too heavy an insert for the book.

The concept of hospitality, kindness, and the threads of fate being inevitable are the main morals of this story.

Skáldskaparmál: The Kidnapping of Idun (Prose Edda)

Three great gods were on a journey through the mountains of Asgard. These gods were Odin, Hœnir, and the trickster, Loki. Through the long passes and days of not eating, they were famished and tired. They came across a herd of Ox and decided to take one for their dinner.

This meat was on the fire for quite some time and no matter how many times they looked to see if it had been cooked, they found it to be just as raw as it had the moment they pulled it off the carcass.

A large eagle was flying up ahead and as Loki looked up to observe it, the eagle spoke. It said that it was using its magic to prevent the meat from cooking, and unless they gave it a portion of the meat, it would not release the spell that bound it. Reluctantly, they agreed. The eagle swooped down and took the best portion of meat available, which angered Loki, as he thought he had been deceived.

Loki proceeded to lunge with a stick at the eagle, but unbeknownst to Loki, this eagle was the giant Thjazi in disguise, and he snatched the stick still being held by Loki and soared high into the sky.

Loki begged the eagle to release him on solid ground, but Thjazi once again required a bargain to be met. The eagle would release Loki only once he swore an oath to kidnap the goddess Idun from her sacred tree in Asgard and bring her, along with her fruits of eternal youth, back to him. Loki agrees once more with reluctance and fear.

Upon the three gods returning home, Loki, honoring his oath in evil deeds, goes to Idun who is always in the vicinity of her precious tree. He tells her of another marvelous tree beyond the wall of Asgard that has fruits even more wondrous than those in Asgard. He tells her to take some of her own fruits and follow him into the forest so she may compare the quality. A trickster indeed! Once they arrive in the false location of the false tree, Idun is surprised by the arrival of the large eagle, being the giant Thjazi, and is kidnapped and taken to his home in the icy mountain realm Thrymheim.

Now, the gods, without their fruits of eternal youth being cared for by the sweet Idun, were beginning to feel the heavy burden of age and frailty. They query with all on the location of

Idun, and it is found that Loki was the last to be seen in her presence. The gods, knowing very well that this was not a good thing, cornered the trickster with all means of threats and pain. When he eventually spoke the truth and told of what had transpired that day in the forest, the gods gave him an ultimatum, to die now or to save poor Idun from her fate.

Generously, the goddess Freyja gave him her cloak of falcon feathers in assistance on his journey, which allowed him to change into a falcon and fly to the far away land. Once he arrived at Jötunheim to retrieve Idun, he saw with delight that Thjazi was out fishing, therefore Loki took the advantage and turned Idun into a nut and flew away with her in his talons back to Asgard.

Thjazi was furious when he found his prize missing. He transformed back into his eagle form and pursued day and night to catch Loki before he could get back into the realm of Asgard. The other gods saw Loki approaching the borders and the eagle close behind, so they got together and built a fire around the fortress. As Loki was just able to avoid the eagle and enter the border, the fire exploded and killed Thjazi instantly.

Here we see the themes of honoring vows and avenging that which was taken.

Scandinavian Folklore

Also called Nordic folklore, these are tales about mythological creatures living in nature, and it encompasses both their Norse mythology and the Christian worldview at the time. These tales are influenced by the folklore of Germany, England, Finland, and the Baltic lands.

These stories were either light and filled with kind creatures who taught the hero a lesson, or dark and scary where an evil being needed to be defeated. Many were told to the children at night or when they were misbehaving to keep them from trouble.

Fairytales from Peter Christen Asbjørnsen and Jørgen Moe have become very popular in our modern era and have been adapted and changed, including some tales by Hans Christian Anderson. The original collection is of around 60 tales called *Popular Tales from the Norse* and was written in the 18th century.

From their lore, we can get a better idea of what the ancient Norse people truly feared or what kind of health and morality issues hung over their heads by interpreting some of these with historical eyes. Let us take a look at some of the interesting creatures behind Scandinavian folklore.

The Huldra

The Huldra, or known in Swedish as the Tallemja, was known to be a beautiful female troll who lived in the woods. Its origins derive from the Norse variation of the story of Adam and Eve, where Eve has to wash and clean all her children when God comes to visit, but those who were unclean before God's arrival would be hidden in the earth from his view forever. Tallemja was the dirty girl who refused to be bathed and escaped her mother's clutch to roam the land instead of being hidden under the ground due to her filthy appearance. These tales were told to scare children so if they were dirty and lied to God about where they had been, their souls would join the other hidden children under the earth forever. We suppose it is a good way to get the children to clean themselves and be truthful.

The Nisse

This was a creature that originally was known to live in the outskirts of every house, in their barns or vicinity, also known as the "household spirit." The Nisse was associated with their winter solstice, and what we would call a Christmas folklore. These creatures look like little garden gnomes but with immense strength, and they guard homes from evil. Often disapproving of bad manners or unkempt farms and animals, it is said that if one spills a drink in their house they must shout a warning to the Nisse who lived under them. A bowl of porridge was given as a sacrificial offering to please the Nisse every Christmas Eve. If the porridge was not there, the Nisse could cause trouble to the house and the animals; therefore, this tradition was practiced to make sure the farm was kept safe and healthy by the Nisse who looked over it. The most treasured of the farm animals by this creature was the horse, and it was said that whichever horse was the healthiest and most beautiful was most likely the favorite of the Nisse, as it would take better care of that animal than the rest.

Pesta

The Pesta was a personification of the Black Death that killed many Scandinavian adults and children during the Medieval Period. Disease was something that took many lives in rural communities in Norway and Denmark.

This figure was portrayed as an old woman wearing a black cloak and red skirt, roaming the country and causing illness and death. It was said that if she was seen carrying a rake near a house, then not all would die and some would pass through the teeth of the rake, thus being spared. But if she was carrying a broom, then it was doom for the whole family. This personification is an attempt at explaining a horrible experience of death due to disease. The path she traveled was a map of where the disease spread, through the countryside, over mountains, and even traveling on boats—this being particularly interesting as the Black Plague was thought to have arrived to the shores of Norway via infected ship rats.

Nokken

Also called a Nixie, this is a monster that takes the humanoid shape of a water creature in Germanic and Scandinavian folktales. The characteristics of the Nokken change depending on the geographical location of the story's origin. For instance, in Norway this monster resides in lakes, rivers, and ponds lurking at the surface and looking out with dark evil eyes. In Sweden, the creature is actually seen as a beautiful man who entices women to jump into the water and then drowning them. Many consider this creature to be related to the mermaid or siren who sings to sailors but with deadly consequences. One of the central attributes of this monster is its capability to shapeshift and therefore take on any form it wishes.

The Draugr

The Draugr is known as a horrendous undead sea monster covered in seaweed and sometimes seen sitting in a rowing boat in the form of an old man. Scandinavian sailors were known to be afraid of the Draugr, who would drown them at sea during storms. If the man appeared in his boat screaming to the sailors, someone was going to drown that night. The term *draugr* in Old Norse means "a ghost or spirit."

Chapter 4: Seiðr, Spà, & Galdr

The magic that was possible in ancient times has probably been diluted to such a degree that we no longer feel a fluid connection to the spiritual world as deeply as they did. The Norse were highly entwined with what was not seen. Magic was a connection not just to a consciousness but to the entirety of the living world. Spirits resided in everything and influenced everyone.

Norse magic revolved around the understanding of things and having a deep knowledge of the methods and techniques needed to perform the art. It most likely took many years to learn how to hear and read the signs around them, remembering the songs and asking the right questions. The Norse people were almost obsessed with the concept of fate, destiny, and the changes of course in one's future. Prophecies and enlightenment on the "way things will be" is what guided everyone from common folk to the elite and the kings. Magic was used in almost everything they did and the one person with the most knowledge on the subject was the most regarded.

These women were known as seers, sorceresses, or *völva*. Depending on the magic used, they are also referred to as *sieðrkona*, *spákona,* or *seiðrfolk*. This art was highly regarded as a women's task, that is, the practice of divination and the speaking to spirits. It was frowned upon if men used magic, as it was seen as unmanly and shameful. Strangely enough, as you might remember from above, Odin himself learned the magic of the runes and is known to practice seiðr, along with his wife Freyja, which is what gives him that shamed, unmanly facet of his theme.

Dreams and their meanings were evaluated and studied too, and they were given great importance. Some dreams were foretelling of doom and death, and some were messages from spirits in other worlds or from ancestors long gone.

The seers would travel the regions and counsel men and their families. They would travel to large events or gatherings and assist in the rituals of sacrifice and worship, prophesy new births, and bless for new unifications. They were brewers of healing potions and casters of curses. They could change the weather or make people fall in love by chanting the Galdr chants and songs.

There are three main branches of the craft: Seiðr-craft, Spá-craft, and Galdr-craft.

Seiðr

A common mistake is to assume that seiðr is the general term for all Norse witchcraft, whereas each magic has a specific branch, form, and use. Seiðr in particular was used as a base for the idea of weaving the threads of fate and destiny, allowing the seer to hear the secrets of the spirits that they called to them and prophesy their benefit or loss.

Seiðr translates from the Old Norse to "string, cord, or snare" and was practiced in Norse society in the later Scandinavian Iron Age. Depending on the need, it was used in blessing the family or cursing the enemy, increasing fertility or crop growth, as well as influencing animals and the weather.

Connection to Shamanism

These women mostly traveled their regions and that of their neighbors, keeping a nomadic lifestyle so they may search for new truths and gain as much knowledge about the world around them. Going from village to village, they performed their magic in return for money or housing for the night.

The act of shamanism comes into play when we see how they induced intricate trance states by meditating and chanting to the spirit realm. The magic was that of illusion and manipulation as well as soul-healing. Partial nudity in these states was common and some connect this type of shamanism to the origins of the pagan witch on a broomstick, flying naked, and chanting around a fire in a group. Women who performed seiðr were usually marginalized in their communities, as this was sometimes seen as dirty or sexually shameful chaos magic, even as it was respected and revered.

Initially connected to the goddess Freyja, it was later also associated with the god Odin (who received the magic of seiðr from Freyja). The influence of Christianity pushed more association of 'good' magic onto male gods and outlawed the use of female worship. The men who performed this magic (and there were even those who took it on professionally too) were called *seiðrmenn*.

Performing

We know that these women always performed on a platform (*hjälle* or "high seat") that was usually covered in fur pillows and placed in the middle of the room. Surrounding the platform would be gifts and food. She would be carrying a distaff, a type of ritualistic stick that symbolized her power, along with pouches or bags filled with various magical items (pieces of bone, stone, or wood) used in the ritual.

The völva would sometimes drink a mead or beer that contained some herbs or intoxicating plants to assist in the ecstatic trance work or burn these as incense. At bigger events or for more critical needs, sometimes the magic was performed with other practitioners to increase the magnetic draw of the spirits.

The point was to seek what was hidden from their base of reality and existence and listen for the answers and actions that needed to be made from the spirits that are drawn in. When one goes into meditation, the brain waves decrease and reach an alpha wavelength state that brings you into a deep calm. Now the völva must have been able to get to that level while at the same time keeping the physical body connected and energetic by moving, spinning, humming deeply, or even just doing breath work. The use of either the excited trance work or the more calm and still meditation probably depended on her personal mood that day or on the type of medium connection she was trying to make.

It is often believed that the witchcraft performed by the völva was surrounded by the invoking of inanimate objects. Often river stones were used in conjunction with steel nails or plates to cause a spark that would tell what the weather was going to be like. The distaff used by the völva in rituals would be adorned with crystals and stones to increase the spiritual connection. Or stones were set into the hilts of swords so warriors could heal wounds that were given when using the weapon. Warriors also used to suck on river stones during battle to ward off thirst and hunger.

Apart from being used to grasp the fates, the seer would use her magic to protect men in battle and ensure their enemies death. Women would perform this war magic to the warriors before they left for war to give them hope, courage, rage, and energy while assuring that the spirits and gods were on their side. Sometimes these women would join the men on their battles and raids to keep the magic 'flowing' and to heal the wounded.

Derivation

Here we read a section from the *Saga of Erik the Red* describing Þórbjörg, the völva who traveled across Greenland revealing her knowledge:

> A high seat was set for her, complete with a cushion. This was to be stuffed with chicken feathers. When she arrived one evening, along with the man who had been sent to fetch her, she was wearing a black mantle with a strap, which was adorned with precious stones right down to the hem. About her neck she wore a string of glass beads on her head and a hood of black lambskin lined with white catskin. She bore a staff with a knob at the top, adorned with brass set with stones on top. About her waist she had a linked charm belt with a large purse. In it she kept the charms which

she needed for her predictions. She wore calfskin boots lined with fur, with long, sturdy laces and large pewter knobs on the ends. On her hands she wore gloves of catskin, white and lines with fur.

When she entered, everyone was supposed to offer her respectful greetings, and she responded according to how the person appealed to her. Farmer Thorkel took this wise woman by the hand and led her to the seat which had been prepared for her. He then asked her to survey his flock, servants and buildings. She had little to say about all of it. That evening tables were set up and food prepared for the seeress. A porridge of kid's milk was made for her and as meat she was given the hearts of all the animals available there. She had a spoon of brass and a knife of ivory shaft, its two halves clasped with brass hands, and the point of which was broken off. (p. 3)

It is important to note that in these accounts we only get an idea of what she wears, what she eats, and where she sits. What is not explained is the actual act—that is how she moved, what she said during the trance, or what she revealed, which is what keeps historians on edge.

Spá

The chief function of a spá-wife or *spákona* was as prophetess. The relationship between the spá magic and that of seiðr are often seen in a similar sense. The main difference between the two could be that the *spákona* derives her power from within (something she already possessed), unlike the *seiðkona* who used the spirit's influence as a middle-man of sorts. Even the word *völva* can be classified under the two magics, as it was found to be used loosely for a woman with the gift of foresight.

Considered the fairest of soul-crafts, the worship of forebears was a respected role in the community and the women who practiced it were too. They were also known to be more accepted by the Christian *seiðmann* during the conversion period.

Connection to the Norns

This type of magic leans more towards welfare-working and psychic sensing. The *spákona* would prophesy the *örlögs* (luck or fate) of men and women in their village or community. The origins of the *örlög* can be directly pulled from the telling of the three Norns, the women who sat at the Urd Well under the World Tree and decided the path of everyone's life. Therefore, in some way these women were able to bypass the usual roots of divination and go right to the source. The *spá-wife* was often also associated with the lesser Norns or *dísir* who would come down from their tree and read the *örlögs* of a newborn's fate.

Practiced with more dignity and favor than what we see of the *seiðrkona* women, this form of magic was inspired by positive connections towards the fates and ancestors. Although there was a reference to the spá-wife performing some kind of trance work, it was more likely to be in the use of *útiseta*, going under the cloak for two days meditating, rather than the ecstatic trance work of the seiðr.

The Wyrd (personal destiny) with which they work was seen as an interconnected mesh of choices and actions. All actions, no matter how small, affect the Wyrd like a pond rippling out in concentric circles. Therefore, it was crucial that the dísir would foretell the child or adult's general direction in life so they were able to get a "general feeling" of what they should strive for and accomplish.

This magic was a part of many of the goddesses' themes in the pantheon and even Odin was said to often need their assistance on matters of foresight. Goddess Frigg/Freyja and the goddess Sif, who is Thor's wife, were noticeable characters who stepped into the shoes of völva.

Performing

The performance of spà magic occurred mainly around times of deaths, births, and the counsel of kings and lords on battle plans connecting to the past, present, and future.

Men of spá magic, known as *þule* (thule), were more accepted in their practice of this divine telling. The term refers to the Old Norse word "to speak" and is sometimes used as a religious title. Both men and women were known to receive an honorary seat and the offerings of food and drink for their efforts.

A special characteristic to the thule's seat is that it may often have been set upon a burial mound. As kings had religious seats of power, so did the thule or *spá-wife* when they spoke, most often seated in a holy place of power like the burial mounds of great ancestors. The mounds were flattened at the top so one could stand or place a chair for the speaker. This was both practical in the sense that the community could hear and see them clearly, as well as symbolic, showing their divine power over the common people and over the hallowed dead who dwelt below. And surely the art was easier to practice when you were in the vicinity of the religious spaces and spirits who live there.

Derivation

From the *Hávamál* verse in the Poetic Edda, we can decipher the use of the known term thule when *Fimbul-þulr* (The Great Thule) tells:

> It is time to speak as a thule, on the thule's seat,
>
> at the Well of Wyrd;

I saw and was silent, I saw and thought,

I listened to the speech of folk;

I heard deeming of runes, and they were not silent of redes,

at the halls of the High One, in the halls of the High One,

thus I heard tell (p. 79)

Galdr

The practice of galdr was by far the most common idea of magic during the medieval time. The origins can be found way back before the Viking Era, and the term *galdr* can be associated with the Germanic word for magic itself!

The term *galdr* in Old Norse means 'spell' or 'incantation,' and it was commonly associated with both men and women.

Connection to the Songs

It was said that to connect to the deep power of the gods and spirits one would chant these songs as spells to assist and empower Viking warriors in battle or deter enemies from harming them. Many of the magic spells chanted in galdr were connected to symbols or staves to heighten their magic and power. Some would also apply these power signs in graphic detail in the air in front of them, on a piece of wood, or on their skins as tattoos.

Certain "words of power" were sung, creating vibrational power in song and used in poetry done alone or in a group, which could have been extremely healing. Sunforms and certain breathing techniques were used to create more intention and focus. Some masters of the songs were known to use the art as a weapon against enemies to blunt swords, soften armor, and even raise giant storms from the sea.

Performing

The spells and incantations, or rather the saying of magic, were chanted for all sorts of occasions and were usually added as an extra element to the practice ritual of seiðr. This is quite a specific type of sorcery, focusing mainly on the characteristic of a high-pitched singing. It is said that the falsetto in which they sang these songs was rather pleasing to the ear as they used a specific meterage called the *galdralag*. Some poems ascribe the use of galdr as more cursing, using the tongue as a tool for destruction.

They could make people sick or even kill them. How they sang and what they sang depended on the situation; whether in celebration or war, the song was performed by both men and women, and was either recited on its own for personal purposes or done in conjunction with reading runes or making herbal potions.

The song did not necessarily have to be vocal; it could indeed also be interpreted as an internal voice. Galdr was also used for practical reasons like in the process of childbirth, where women would sing the songs to assist in the delivery of the child, which gave courage to the mother and helped control her breath. The same can be applied to when chanting with the rune divination where one would either do it internally, as imagining the sound, or externally, therefore vocalizing each sound—

breathing into the nostrils and holding the breath in your naval center, which is the source of life-force energy, as you chant out the first rune in a drawn out syllable for syllable. Fehu, for instance, would be sung as "Feeeeeeeeh-huuuuuu," each syllable being the exhale from the naval center in a deep tone.

Often understood to be performed in an informal and impromptu setting that would better activate the magic and incantation, the vocalizing of the spells is what was thought to make it more potent. Unfortunately, there are not many surviving artifacts from the Medieval Period of actual spells performed, but there is a vast amount of mentions of these incantations being performed and sung.

Derivation

Various galdr songs can be found in the *Grógaldr* or the Spells of Gróa.

There was the use of galdr in the necromantic practice of Svipdag's attempt to bring his mother Groá, a völva, back from the grave. Groá had requested this of her son if he may ever need her assistance or guidance.

Here we see a reference to galdr in the poem *Skirnismál* in the Poetic Edda where Skirnir, the messenger of Frey, goes to the giantess Gerðor and sings this galdr so that she may fall in love with Frey.

Heyri jötnar,	Give heed, frost-rulers,
heyri hrímÞursar,	hear it, giants.
sybir Suttungs,	Sons of Suttung,
sjakfir ásliðar,	And gods, ye too,
hvé ek fyrbýð,	How I forbid
hvé ek fyrirbanna	and how I ban
manna glaum mani,	The meeting of men with the maid,
manna nyt mani.	(The joy of men with the maid). (stanza 34)

Chapter 5: Runes & Runestones

Runes were first thought to appear around the 1st century and uncertainty still surrounds their place of origin. '*Rún*' in Old Norse means 'symbol,' 'letter,' or 'character.' In some cases, the translation points towards the word r*uno*, being a 'mystery' or a secret of sorts. Like many of the other characteristics of Norse culture, absorption of external influences was most likely the creation of the language in the first place.

The shape that developed for each rune was a pragmatic one. Firstly, parchment and inks were expensive and hard to come by, which meant carving onto already available materials from nature was more practical. Straight vertical lines, rather than the curved letters, were easier to carve with tools into tough surfaces.

The resemblance to the Egyptian hieroglyphs gives the language a very perplexing image to those accustomed to the Latin alphabet. One character can represent various sounds and at the same time also represent whole words or phrases. Characters could be read left to right, right to left, and top to bottom without the use of spacing, making a runologist's job quite tough. We suppose the fact that it's a lot less straightforward to decipher is probably what makes the job so interesting to begin with!

The original runic inscriptions in Elder Futhark were carved onto materials that held significance, therefore elevating the status of the object itself. Their use varied depending on the need, and the materials on which they were carved varied just the same. Wood, iron, stone, and bone each held an inert power and influence over the runes themselves.

The Norse were not technically illiterate, as is the misconception, and most people could read and carve runes, or at least knew the basic inscriptions. They were simply more interested in using the runes to tell stories, give personal messages, and express love rather than record their daily practices and rituals with more detail. The passing on of their detailed knowledge to the next generation was mostly oral.

Archaeologists have found these ancient inscriptions most famously on the large runestones, but also in cliff walls and around sacred groves and waterfalls where offerings and worship took place. Runes were used as trade markers for merchants detailing their goods or were carved near grave mounds and on other religious objects. Runes were carved on pieces of wood to send messages to family and people in neighboring villages or even as graffiti when people just passed through the village. Riddles and various jokes are also found on runestones, with a plentiful number of love letters to women and dead relatives as well.

Runes were often carved into and around the house walls, into various house items and accessories such as combs, around mirrors, on the sole of shoes, on plate ware, and carved onto pendants and pieces of clothing. Protection in battle was a straightforward need; therefore, finding protective runes on weapons, helmets, and shields was commonplace.

Some of these inscriptions also bore the interaction they had with other cultures. For instance, the runic inscription, "love conquers all," which was originally a Latin phrase from the poet Virgil, had somehow passed into their society and took form through runic inscriptions.

The use of runes before the Christianization of the Scandinavian kingdoms was more practical than divine. Even though some small accounts do attest to the use of runes for divination in the sagas of the Poetic Edda, most were largely for protection and practical use.

Odin's Gift

Throughout the many sagas and poems surrounding the gods and heroes of Norse mythology, it is comprehensible that the idea of sacrificing something important to the main character in return for knowledge and power is a key element. The ultimate sacrifice was the one of self-sacrifice. We see the original theme in the poem *Hávamál* from the Poetic Edda, in which we experience Odin's challenge and strife from his own perspective.

The great Odin, sitting on his throne, is hungry for the wisdom of all things. He decides to venture in search of this mighty wisdom at Mímir's Well, where he sacrifices his eye and throws himself onto his own spear, Gungnir, all in the name of the quest. Here he only receives half of the knowledge he requires, therefore, he still ventures forth in search of more.

From his throne in Asgard, he looks out at the Norns by their well below Yggdrasil and sees their power in weaving and threading the fates of all beings. So, Odin takes it upon himself to learn their magic, but in order for him to receive the knowledge of the magic of the fates he again has to sacrifice something. So, self-wounded by a spear, he hangs in the tree for nine days and nights, looking into the pool and denying any assistance from the other gods.

> I know that I hung on a wind rocked tree,
>
> nine whole nights, with spear wounded,
>
> and to Odin offered myself to myself;
>
> on that tree of which no one knows from what root it springs.
>
> Bread no one gave me, no horn of drink,
>
> downward I peered, to runes applied myself,

> wailing learnt them, then fell down thence. (*Hávamál*, stanza 138)

Finally! The runes had revealed themselves to him through visions and secrets. But he is not the same as he was; he has changed and been reborn. The symbolism that half of Odin's self had died in that tree and that he came out of the ordeal a stronger being is the idea of passing the physical limits of the mortal self to arrive at the divine and immortal.

> Then I fertilized and became wise;
>
> I truly grew and thrived.
>
> From a word to a word I was led to a word,
>
> From a work to a work I was led to a work. (stanza 163)

From there he uses his gained knowledge to pass on the runes to the men of the world so they may be able to learn and grow like he did.

Myth aside, what the evidence tells us is that historically, Germanic tribes often warred and traded with Roman people in the south and eventually brought back with them to Scandinavian kingdoms their own take on the Old Italic language, molding it and altering it to their own worldview, thus creating the Elder Futhark.

Elder Futhark

This is the original and oldest used language of the Scandinavian region, which appeared in the 1st century during the Dark Ages, also called the Germanic Futhark.

The name Futhark actually derives from the first six letters of their alphabet (ᚠ☒þ☒☒☒).

☒ - fehu   ☒ - naubiz   ☒ - ehwaz

☒ - uruz   I - isa   ☒ - mannaz

þ - burisaz   ☒ - jera   ☒ - laguz

☒ - ansuz   ☒ - eihwaz   ☒ - inguz

☒ - raido   ☒ - perb   ☒ - dagaz

☒ - kaunaz   ᛉ - algiz   ☒ - opala

⌾ - gebo   ⌾ - sowilo

⌾ - wunjo   ⌾ - tiwaz

⌾ - hagalaz   ⌾ - berkana

Since the names in these runes are not preserved anywhere in Elder Futhark, historians have had to try and reconstruct them from the names preserved in the later runic alphabets, almost like retracing steps of language. The Gothic alphabet is the earliest available Germanic language in large cohesive texts from 300 C.E. when the names of the letters in the alphabet were based on runes.

Another adaptation of the writing system came from the Anglo-Saxon (Old English) texts in the 5th century, creating the Anglo-Frisian Futhorc. Consisting of between 24 and 33 characters, this version was used by Frisian (Germanic group of Netherlands and Denmark) cultures and brought to England as seen in the use of manuscripts. This lasted until the late 11th century before being supplanted by the Latin alphabet.

Although very rare in the Viking Age, and mostly seen in the proto-Norse migration period, bind-runes were used as a ligature of two or more runes. They were either a simple two rune (rarely three) combination to make a single conjoined glyph. Then the same-stave rune, which is a larger conglomeration of runes, stemmed together and was usually found on runestones.

There are two choices one needs to make when transcribing from modern English to Runic: either you write it as a direct letter for rune translation, which might not come out as it would be pronounced (but how it is spelt), or you write it phonetically (as it's pronounced) which removes or changes the placement of runic letters accordingly. There are no runic alphabet letters that are equivalent to all the 26 letters or to all the sounds used in English today.

Younger Futhark

The Elder Futhark slowly underwent a reform in the late 7th century and 8 out of the 24 characters were eventually removed. This established the 16-character Younger Futhark of the Viking Age, also called the Scandinavian Futhark.

Some serious changes occurred to the language as vowels were added and characters removed. Therefore, one could see a trend towards a more minimalistic and useful form of the language where diplomatic and trade orientated subjects could be expressed. These changes included some distinct sounds that were written the same.

ᚠ - Fé   ᚼᚼ - Hagall   ᛒᛒ - Bjarkan

ᚢ - Úr   ᚾᚾ - Nauðr   ᛘᚢ - Maðr

þ - Thurs   l - Is   ᛚ - Logr

ᚬ - As/Oss   ᛅᛅ - Ar   ᛦ - Yr

ᚱ - Reið   ᛋ' - Sol

ᚴ - Kaun   ᛏᛏ - Tyr

A further division went under way in the Younger Futhark, splitting into the long-branch Danish runes, which were better used for documenting information on stone, and the short-twig (Rök) runes, which were thought to be a shorthand for personal messages on wood. They originated in the Swedish and Norwegian cultures.

Some runes were adapted even further and lacked the normal strokes and lines used in the Younger Futhark. These runes were called Hälsinge Runes or staveless runes, meaning they lack the 'stave' or stroke—something like a "budget rune."

Rune Poems

Rune poems are the top source of relevance to the Younger Futhark's 16-letter alphabet. They provide for their user an explanation of each runic letter in a poetic stanza to help remember pronunciation and relevance for each rune. Each of these rune poems has a couple of lines giving memorable images to help remember the name of the rune.

They are divided into three parts: Norwegian Rune Poems, Icelandic Rune Poems, and Anglo-Saxon Rune Poems. Norwegian and Icelandic poems were based on the Younger Futhark, while the Anglo-Saxon used the relevant Anglo-Saxon Runic alphabet.

Due to the sheer amount of information on each region's version of the poems, we will provide the most well systematized of the three: the Icelandic Rune Poems of the 15th century.

- ᚠ - Fé (Wealth)

    Fé er frænda róg   Source of discord among kinsmen

    ok flæðar viti   and fire of the sea

    ok grafseiðs gata   and path of the serpent

    aurum fylkir.

- ᚢ - Úr (Shower)

    Úr we skýja grátr   Lamentation of the clouds

    ok skára þverrir   and ruin of the hay-harvest

    ok hirðis hatr.   and abomination of the shepherd.

    umbre visi

- Þ - Thurs (Giant)   *Þurs er kvenna kvöl*   The torturer of women

    ok kletta búi   and cliff-dweller

> *ok varðúðar verr.*   and husband of a giantess.
>
> *Saturnus þengill.*

- ᚬ - As/Óss (God)

  > *Óss er algingautr*   Aged Gautr
  >
  > *ok ásgarðs jöfurr,*   and prince of Asgard
  >
  > *ok valhallar vídi.*   and lord of Valhalla.

- ᚱ - Reið (Riding)

  > *Reið er sitjandi sæla*   Joy of the horsemen
  >
  > *ok snúðig ferð*   and speedy journey
  >
  > *ok jórs erfiði.*   and toil of the steed.
  >
  > *iter ræsir.*

- ᚴ - Kaun (Ulcer)

  > *Kaun er barna böl*   Disease fatal to children

> *ok bardaga för*   and painful spot
>
> *ok holffúa hús.*   and abode of mortification.
>
> *flagella konungr.*

- 🇭 - Hagall (Hail)

  > *Hagall er kaldakorn*   Cold grain
  >
  > *ok krapadrífa*   and shower of sleet
  >
  > *ok snáka sótt.*   and sickness of serpents.
  >
  > *grando hildingr.*

- 🇳 - Nauðr (Constraint)

  > *Nauð er þýjar þrá*   Grief of the bone-maid
  >
  > *ok þungr kostur*   and state of oppression
  >
  > *ok vássamlig verk.*   and toilsome work.
  >
  > *opera niflungr.*

- I - Ís (Ice)

Íss er árbörkr   Bark of rivers

ok unnar þak   and roof of the wave

ok feigra manna fár.   and destruction of the doomed.

glacies jöfurr.

- ᛡᛡ - Ár (Plenty)

   Ár er gumna góði   Boon to men

   ok gott sumar   and good summer

   algróinn akr.   and thriving crops.

   annus allvaldr

- ᛡ' - Sól (Sun)

   Sól er skýja skjöldur   Shield of the clouds

   ok ísa aldrtregi.   and shining ray

   rota siklingr.   and destroyer of ice.

- ᛡᛡ - Týr

> *Týr er einhendr áss*   God with one hand
>
> *ok ulfs leifar*   and leaving of the wolf
>
> *ok hofa hilmir.*   and prince of temples.
>
> *Mars tiggi.*

- ᛒ - Bjarkan (Birch)

  > *Bjarkan er laufgat lim*   Leafy twig
  >
  > *ok lítit tré*   and little tree
  >
  > *ok ingsamligr viðr.*   and fresh young shrub.
  >
  > *abies buðlungr.*

- ᛘ - Maðr (Man)

  > *Maðr er manns gaman*   Delight of man
  >
  > *ok moldar auki*   and augmentation of the earth
  >
  > *ok skipa skreytir.*   and adorner of ships.

homo mildingr.

- ᛚ - Lögr (Water)

    Lögr er vallanda vatn
                        Eddying stream

    *ok viðr ketil*l   and broad geysir

    ok glömmungr grundi.   and land of the fish.

    lacus lofðungr.

- ᛦ - Ýr (Yew)

    Ýr er bendr bogi   Bent bow

    ok brotgjarnt járn   and brittle iron

    ok fífu fáarbauti.   and giant of the arrow.

    arcus ynglingr.

What we see here is the relevance of each poem to the theme and character of each rune. Just like one would sing rhymes to children to help them learn English and word association, this too was used as a method of learning and remembrance. The stress put on the first syllable of the word is what makes it complicated to relate to modern English. Norse poetry alliterates the first letter of the word whereas English normally uses rhyming of the last letter of the word.

Icelandic Rune Staves

With the settlement of Norse people in Iceland around 870 C.E., the Younger Futhark alphabet was taken with them and further adapted for magical purposes. This can be seen as a conglomeration of different characters to wield more powers. You would find three or more runes combined into an intricate character that possessed combined magic and meaning.

The use of this white magic was known as Galdrasafur, meaning "magical stick" or 'stave,' and it was practiced more by men in Iceland. They were carved, like other Nordic runes, on specific materials and influenced a certain effect or outcome. A small drop of blood was also used as a personal sacrifice to the magic. Being very specific and relevant to what the Icelanders needed at the time, their magic was used as a tool to kill an enemy's cattle, for increased fertility, "to guide through bad weather or bring victory during competitions of wrestling, called glíma," (Iceland Rovers, 2017). Some were used to help with fishing or rowing your boat, the healing of fox bites, or even to make your sheep more docile.

We see that in the middle of the 16th century the outlaw of runes was heavily forced and many men were put to death for still having an intimate relationship with their pagan religion and use of runes around their abodes.

The most common runic staves used were:

- *Aegishjálmur*, "Helm of Awe," had the shape of a four or an eight to form an equal cross with branches at its terminals. Here we see the saga of Sigurd who slays the great serpent Fáfnir in order to win a treasure horde of the Niflungs. Part of the treasure is the symbol of *Aegishjálmur,* which surrounded him in an ethereal way with power and protection. It was named Solomons Innsigil once Christianity took hold.
- *Að unni* was a simplified version of the complex symbol of *Aegishjálmur,* with fewer branches, used mainly as a love

stave. So, a man might find the love of a woman. This symbol was most often drawn with one's own spit in their right hand.
- Another to consider is the *Hraethigaldur*, a stave used to put fear on an enemy. Carved on some bark and worn as a pendant, this would keep your enemies at a distance and fearful of you. But always make sure you see your enemy before he sees you!

Runestones

Runestones had one main purpose: to be seen! They are large upright slabs of stone displaying various messages, poems, and life stories of the person or family the rune was about. The runes were often painted with bright colors and sometimes accompanied by elaborate drawings depicting scenes of battle or triumph. Both men and women commissioned runestones and were often used to elevate their social standing within the community. Most of the runestones still standing today are located in Sweden, but many more can be found across the other Scandinavian regions like Denmark and Norway, as well as the locations where Vikings traveled during their raids and trades.

The use of runic inscriptions on large stones and bedrock started in the 4th century and lasted till the 12th century when the Viking Age was at a close.

Interesting fact: Most runestones were actually carved by the converted Norse people during the Viking Era, which was right in the middle of a religious conversion, and so many of the carvings were about Christian stories, depicting crosses and invoking the name of their new God. This was probably to show their neighbors how well they had converted to the new religion and forsaken their pagan past.

Tools Used

It was quite important that the runes were carved correctly; they needed to be on the appropriate surface and location be sure that they invoked the correct deity for their chosen purpose. Bad luck and ill fortune would be your burden if you did not complete the process with care.

Carving runestones must have been a rather arduous job to complete when they worked on large stone slabs that were later erected as runestones. But for smaller objects that had personal meaning, it was a quick and manageable task done with skill and experience.

The tools used to carve the horizontal and vertical lines were:

- Chisels: Easy to make and fairly cheap, the chisel was normally a metal stick of sorts, easily held in the palm of one's hand. Blunted on one end to allow contact with the hammer and pointed on the other to create indentations on the surface of the material, the runemaster would drive the chisel into the wood or stone with a certain amount of force. It required a deft and experienced hand or the stone would chip and crack with too much pressure from the hammer, or the wood would split and splinter causing the incorrect indentations needed. Imagine having to re-do a whole piece of work because you incorrectly chiseled the last few rune inscriptions on the block!
- Hammer: Either wooden or metal, hammers were also a rather cheap and

common tool. The hammer was used to smash down on the chisel and create enough force to cause an indentation on the surface. Runemasters had to be very careful to not crack the entire stone or injure themselves badly with lack of precision. Hammers could break and chisels could go blunt, therefore, the tools were often repaired and replaced to keep the quality of the work up to standard.

Where They Stand

Mainly found in large crossroads, waterways, and property boundaries, these stones were placed for easy observation by whomever passed by. The names of the runes are mostly associated with their location to the towns they are situated in.

There are over 2,500 runestones found in Sweden, more than the other Nordic countries, and this is due to their earlier conversion to Christianity.

- The Ramsund carving in Sweden is found on a rocky outcrop next to a bridge and thought to have been carved in the

10th century. It is not necessarily considered a runestone per se, as it was not found elevated and standing but rather just depicted on a flat rock. It is thought to have been commissioned by a prominent Norse woman who inscribed her family's names into the rock and added mighty gods to the rune associating them with favor and good fortune. This was carved in Younger Futhark.
- Jelling runestones in Denmark show two standing stones from the 10th century memorializing two generations of a royal Danish family. One from a king called Gorm the Old, memorializing his wife, and the other from his son Harold Bluetooth after Gorems death. This too was carved in Younger Futhark.
- The Rök runestone is by far the most famously known to this day. Located in Sweden, it marks the initial stage of Swedish literature and consists of poetry of tautology (statements that tell of ideas and thoughts). Before it was moved to a new position, this stone was part of a medieval church dated to the 9th century and carved in Elder Futhark.

- The Einang runestone is found in Norway and was also initially part of a church building. This stone has been dated all the way to the 4th century and has been thought to be the earliest finding of the term 'rune' in Elder Futhark.
- The Varangian runestones are located in over 30 places in Scandinavian and Europe. They attest to the voyages of the Varangian guard from the east into Russia, to the Baltic, and into Greece and Italy.

The placement of the various runestones found in Eastern and Western Europe is almost like a dotted map, showing just how far their reach really went—in the Baltic lands near waterways or in towns in Southern Europe.

Reading the Stones

These professional carvers used a basic layout to follow: starting with a name of the commissioner of the stone, next would be the name of the person who died and what they had realized during their life, then a prayer, and the name of the carver. This demonstrates that rune carvers were quite literate and often chiseled short, to the point messages on these stones.

Most were carved in Younger Futhark and it can be challenging to pinpoint the sound used for each character, as they had so many versions.

We can also see many tender and romantic stories told about a lover's death and their memory. For instance, the runestone raised by a farmer named Holmgöt attests his love for his wife and that there was no better woman to help him on the farm than her. This runestone was placed over his wife's grave.

Runemasters

Runestones were often carved by non-professional runecarvers like merchants, farmers, and Vikings as depictions of daily life. Later in the 11th century, professional runemasters were coming to prominence who solely focused on the carving of commissions given by the family or person it related to. The runemasters would appoint apprentices to assist in the commissions, as it became a very profitable and work intensive job. The runemaster often also needed to be a proficient stonesman, as it was very difficult to select and carve correctly on the large stone blocks.

Chapter 6: Runic Divination

When we talk about using runes for divination, it must be specified that the magic used is that of the mind and that of the soul, not to be confused with fortune-telling. The pieces of stone or wood with symbols on them are not what contain the power to detect obstacles and great events in your future. The magic comes from the strength of human will and the intention of seeing a possible path, not an answer! "It's about looking for possible causes and effects and seeing potential outcomes," (Newcombe, 2019).

The practice of runic divination during the Viking Age has been in question for many years. Findings in Icelandic Sagas do mention the use of runes in some kind of divination, such as the *Ynglinga Saga* from the Icelandic poet Snorri Sturluson, where a king recites his visit to the temple in Uppsala: "the chips fell in a way that said that he would not live long," (stanza 40). This could easily be interpreted as the use of runic divination, but the accounts are so small and varied that it is best to acknowledge the current idea of divination before the end of the Viking Era as negligible due to it being a late adaptation during the 13th century. Therefore, historians have not directly linked divination with rune casting prior to the Christianization of Scandinavia. Thus, could it really be considered authentic?

New ideas and patterns that are brought into the runes over the centuries should not be ostracized because they didn't apply to the ancient practices of the past, but rather be acknowledged in an esoteric way to each user. Adding or interchanging meaning with each person's personal beliefs is not a sin. We are sure that none of the Norsemen are turning in their graves just because you didn't say the word right or used the symbol in the correct way. The point is that you are using the threads of fate to guide you through the rush and rumble of the modern world so you may open your soul to the influences of past, future, and present. That is what the idea of paganism was, a very personalized variant.

The Three Ættir

Æett, or Ættir for plural, means family, clan, or group, and Elder Futhark is the runic language used to create these Ættir's. The division of the three gods watching over each Æett reflects the various social divisions of tribal society: the nurturer, the priest, and the warrior. What these Ættir's are to each rune is a theme using an ancient separation of writings and codes. Each Æett is technically the narrator of the story depending on its use and meaning, and they will change the perspectives of runes to fit the theme and relate emotions specific for each Æett. Some of these runes can be read in reverse to mean the exact opposite, most often negatively.

Each Ætt is a splitting of the Elder Futhark into three equal parts of eight runes each. Natural elements are used as themes and can belong to two or three of the Æetts at the same time and thus overlap and emphasize more meaning to each character. Love for The Mother, wisdom for The King, or rage for The Warrior.

The Mother

This is known to be the Ættir of Freyr, son of god Njord and ruler of peace. Some interchange the god with the goddess Freyja, his sister, who also holds the virtues for this Æett. The Mother symbolizes sex, intimacy, benefactor for cultivation of crops, fertility, passion, interpersonal relations, physical touch, care, and, most importantly, the function of nurturer. This Æett often refers to the color green.

The runes falling under Freyr's Ætt are:

- ᚠ Fehu (Cattle)

    This indicates material wealth, prosperity, hope, and luck. The symbol signifies cattle, which was their main source of livelihood at the time, resonating with the ideal of wealth.

- ᚢ Uruz (Ox)

    This indicates strength, hard work, and motivation. The symbol signifies the ox, which is known to persevere and be a symbol of intense masculinity.

- Þ Thurisaz (Mallet)

This indicates challenge and conflict. The symbol signified Thor's hammer/mallet or the symbol of giant, which indicated the will of energy and power of destruction.

- ⍑ Ansuz (Message)

    This indicates communication—a divine message or wisdom, truth, and inspiration. It's connected to the god Odin, his visions, and good advice.

- ⍑ Raidho (Journey)

    This indicates the movement of a wheel in the cycle of life and the spiritual journey each person has to go through; the physical quest of venturing forth.

- ⍑ Kenaz (Torch)

    This indicates the unknown and what needs to come to light. The symbol represents a torch for finding the secrets and the true calling of your path.

- ⍑ Gebo (Gift)

This indicates partnership and generosity. The symbol signifies the gift of understanding balance.

- ᚹ - Wunjo (Joy)

    This indicates the ideal of joy, celebration, peace, and harmony. The symbol signifies the comfort and joy of others in your life.

The King

This is known to be the Ættir of Heimdall, who was the watchmen of the gods. Symbolizing shamanism, diplomacy, and guardianship, we see the function of a priest and the connection between life, death, and magic. This Æett is often depicted in the color grey.

The runes falling under Heimdall's Ætt are:

- ᚺ Hagalaz (Hail)

    This indicates a natural form of disaster. The symbol signifies hail and shows the unavoidable cost that nature brings which is out of our control. But the lesson to be learned is that we weather the storm and move forward with grace.

- ᚾ Nauthiz (Needs)

    This indicates the time spent maintaining survival and recuperating from the long day. The symbol signifies restriction, disagreement, and practicing patience.

- ᛁ Isa (Ice)

    This indicates the feeling of being stuck in a situation in life. It was symbolized to gather all information and patiently await the next move, avoid frustration, and keep a level head.

- ᛃ Jera (Harvest)

    This indicates the reaping and conclusion of hard work, symbolizing the need to show gratitude for what has come to pass and be ready for the next step.

- ᛇ - Eihwaz (Yew)

    This indicates the reference to Yggdrasil, the Tree of The World. It symbolizes reliability, the trustworthiness of things, and a sense of purpose.

- ⚈ - Perthro (Destiny)

    This indicates fortune and chance, symbolizing the ideal of making life fateful by taking what you receive with open arms and open heart; the mysteries and fates in a roll of dice.

- ᛉ - Algiz (Elk)

    This indicates the protection and defense of the family. Symbolizing guardianship and courage, one must manifest their dreams and shield their Wyrd from the evil of negative emotions.

- ⚈ - Sowilo (Sun)

    This indicates happiness and success, symbolizing the celebration of reaching goals and keeping the body in optimal health.

The Warrior

This is known to be the Ættir of Tyr, the sky god who stood for war and justice. Symbolizing strength and bravery, law and honor, service and loyalty, and a legacy left behind, this Æett is often depicted in the color red.

The runes falling under Tyr's Ætt are:

- ⟨ᛏ⟩ - Tiwaz (Victory)

    This indicates direction as symbolized by the arrowhead of Tyr. Leadership and victory while knowing your true strengths and weaknesses were the ideal of rationality.

- ⟨ᛒ⟩ - Berkana (Birch)

    This indicates the ideal of regeneration, both physical and spiritual. The Birch goddess oversaw new beginnings and the creation of growth, symbolizing renewal.

- ⟨ᛖ⟩ - Ehwaz (Horse)

This indicates the need for a trusty assistant like the horse, which was the only transport at the time. It symbolized the steady progress and teamwork needed to accomplish tasks and goals.

- ᛗ - Mannaz (Man)

    This indicates the social order of humanity and personal identity, symbolized by the ideals of cooperation, relationships, and eventual mortality.

- ᛚ - Laguz (Lake)

    This indicates the emotion factor of intuition and fluidity. Symbolized by the element of water, it has powers of renewal but also holds mysteries and secrets.

- ᛜ - Ingwaz (Fertility)

    This indicates the Earth god Ing, symbolizing well-being, virtue, strength, and family.

- ᛟ - Othala (Heritage)

    This indicates the ideal of inheritance, symbolizing the legacy of one's name and the values one needs to live by to live an abundant life.

- ᛞ - Dagaz (Dawn)

This indicates consciousness and clarity, symbolizing the transformative power of change and the ideals of hope and security.

Casting

Strong human intention is the key to activating the magic, and the power is in the human, not the inanimate object.

Casting has been practiced for centuries and is still widely used today. Reading what was cast was not a fortune-telling magic but rather the concept of looking for answers and guidance in future outcomes. Placing energy and will power into the runes before reading is done too.

This oracular divination method requires the person to use critical thinking and basic intuition by asking certain questions to the fates and looking for the answer in the past, present, and future. Making runes was known as risting and it entailed carving onto pieces of bark from nut bearing trees or using smooth river stones and crystals. The making of runes is said to be just as important as the casting themselves therefore taking care in the magical process.

Traditionally, runes could be cast in two different ways: placing a white piece of fabric on the floor and casting the runes while looking into the skies and selecting the runes to allow the fates to fall into place, or throw the runes and only read the ones that are shown upright. Some use this base fabric or leather, but it could also be cast directly on the floor or surface. Another option is to ask a yes or no question to the universe and select blindly from the runes in the pouch, whichever you receive in your right hand will be the guidance you are looking for.

How you decide to read them is really about personal perspective, but there are some traditional methods used that could be interpreted differently depending on the personal method.

The Ætt in Casting

One can say that for each rune there is a symbol, for example the symbol of light in Freyr's Ætt, that is ken, is the torch, and for Heimdall it is sowilo. As well as the referral of wealth and achievement, you will see that it reflects in Freyr's Fehu, in Heimdall's Nauthiz, and in Tyr's Tiwaz.

It is important to see that at the end of each Ætt the rune used is always a positive and hopeful one, like Sowilo as Sun and Dagaz as Dawn. This symbolized the end of the lesson and the venture onto new challenges.

What you might also notice is how the overlapping of some themes do not reflect in the third Ætt, like death, found in Perthro in Heimdall's Ætt and Raidho in Freyr's Ætt. Tyr's Ætt does not indicate this theme, telling us that maybe the warrior had already come to learn all those lessons and moved to the next stage, where Freyr and Heimdall still need to make choices.

Casting runes is a sacred tool; therefore, it is important to remember that reading too deeply into what is shown might not reflect directly with something happening in your life. It could be subversive and miscellaneous, so keeping a positive attitude towards what is presented is vital.

Rune Spreads

There are many different ways to spread runes in reading for divination, from the two-rune layout to the more complex 24-rune layout.

It is said that before casting one should close their eyes and mix the runes carefully inside the pouch or box in which you keep them safe. This is to allow the flow of past, present, and future within the user's Wyrd. The runes will answer your question in a way that you personally can comprehend. As we said before, there is no "right way" to practice runic divination as long as the user understands that it is a light shining on your path to the answers, not on the direct answers given.

Your rune casts can also be recorded in a way for you to look back at what was shown the previous day, week, or month and see if the tides of fate are falling in your favor.

One, Two, and Three-Rune Layouts

These are the most basic options for calling the runes to your needs:

- The one-rune layout is an interpretation and general feeling of the question asked

when you pick one single rune from the pouch. You would mentally or verbally ask your question, and whichever rune is chosen blindly from your pouch will give you the direction of your answer.
- The two-rune layout represents the ancient Germanic ideal of a twofold concept of time, for "that which is" and "that which is becoming." The first rune picked is the rune of "that which is," enlightening you on the path that you are already walking on. The second pick is "that which is becoming," which could reveal that unseen chance for you to change your path, so you may adhere to what is shown.
- The three-rune layout requires you to select and place three runes next to each other on the fabric in front of you. Each of the three you chose signifies a different stage or answer. The first being the general idea and overview of your question, the second in line being the challenges you face with such a question, and the third is the possible outcomes coming from that question.

Four-Rune Layout

This is a placement of the four runes in a cross formation in front of you. Each position of the rune is related to the north, west, east, and south location of the dwarves: Nordi, Vestro, Austri, and Surdi, who in mythology hold up the sky of Ymir's skull. The first rune placed in the north position in front of you is signifying the past relation to your question. The west rune signifies the present relation to your question. The east rune stands for the future obstacles that may hinder your path, and the southern position stands for the possible outcome of your cast.

It is important to note that the third rune does not predict any future; it simply predicts the future obstacles in your way while the fourth is the typical "future position" of standard layouts.

Five-Rune Layout

One could also move onto a five-rune layout in which you would pick and place these runes into the shape of a cross with the fifth rune in the center. The far left rune indicates the influence of problems, the top rune shows the influence of solutions and positivity, and the bottom indicates the overall influence of the question. The far right is an immediate answer and the middle is the future of what the question might bring.

Seven-Rune Layout

These spreads can be altered according to preference but we will (for practical purposes) list the two main spreads that are known.

You can opt for the V-shape formation in front of you called the Runic V. Starting from the top left, the meanings follow as such: top left shows the past influence, the next down shows present influences, then future actions, followed by the best actions for positive outcome. Moving upwards towards the right, we see the influence of emotions related to the question, followed by possible problems encountered with the question, and finally, top right is the future outcome of the question.

Or, you can opt for the serpent layout where the runes are placed in a flowing formation that guides you from the head to tail of events coming your way. The snaking represents the up and down hills and the path in which you walk along life. It is sometimes referred to as the Serpent of Midgard spread. Let's picture the seven runes snaking one after the other in front of you, beginning from the tail to the head:

- The first rune can represent the feelings you had in the past relating to the question asked.
- The second rune can be read as the struggles and bumps you will face on the journey to the outcome.
- The third rune points towards our concerns at the present time while we take the journey.
- On the fourth rune we can begin to acknowledge our journey towards an outcome even though there is still some way to go.
- The fifth tells us about our feelings once we can begin to see the outcome at hand.
- The sixth rune is a reminder of the struggles ahead even though the outcome is visible.
- And the final rune is the representation of the goal at hand. This goal can be deceiving though, because just like the Serpent of Midgard that bites its own tail, if you are not careful enough when reading the previous runes, you could

end up finding yourself right back at the beginning again.

24-Rune Layout

A much larger 24-rune layout can be read by placing it in a 3 x 8 grid, exemplifying the runic year. This is usually done on New Year's Day to provide answers for the entire year. Read from the top down each of the three columns. They could be interpreted as such:

Row One
- First: how to receive money and prosperity
- Second: how to achieve physical health and strength
- Third: how to achieve defense or destruction
- Fourth: how to achieve wisdom and inspiration
- Fifth: what the direction of your life-path is
- Sixth: what your future wisdom is
- Seventh: skills to be achieved
- Eighth: how to achieve happiness and peace

Row Two
- First: the future changes in your life
- Second: what is needed to achieve these goals
- Third: what obstacles might come your way
- Fourth: your success and achievements
- Fifth: what choices are made and challenges to come
- Sixth: the manifestation of inner skill
- Seventh: situations of life and death
- Eighth: the energy that guides you

Row Three
- First: concerning affairs of a legal nature
- Second: achieve growth and beauty
- Third: your friendships and relationships
- Fourth: your social status
- Fifth: your emotional status
- Sixth: the influences of emotion and sex

- Seventh: your achievement of balance
- Eighth: what wisdom and assets will be gained in the year

The Blank Rune

There is quite a bit of controversy surrounding the use of Odin's Rune. This rune was not as commonly used in traditional rune reading but was later introduced in the 19th century. When drawn from the pouch, it can either be read as a matter of allowing things to just stay secret and unknown or a connection to the fates, destiny, and the knowledge of what is hidden. Some, when presented with Odin's Rune, will simply choose to recast.

"There are many different schools of thought on if to use the blank rune or not in casting. The rune can be a sign that you need to really think about who is the master in your dream" (Auntyflo, 2021).

Chapter 7: Religion

Unlike Christianity, Norse religion is a folk religion. Partaking in a more survivalist and socially focused worship to their many gods, it was often spoken of as the Ásaturu (worship of gods and spirits). The various trans-cultural diffusions between the Sami and Finns, who were their closest neighbors, was most likely what made up their old Norse customs, which were the closest things to religion as a concept at the time. It was animistic, polytheistic, pantheistic (the universe is the manifestation of the deities), and held a cyclical view of time.

The heathen religion was closely related to the different practices performed for different events or gatherings to praise a god according to the theme (war, wealth, health, or fertility). Again, it is vital to understand that because there are not many details regarding their worship, it is suggested that we make an unclear image of interpretations from what survived. What we do know is that the Norse did not put up too much of a fight towards the new religion, because in their polytheistic culture and worshiping a long list of gods, adding Christ to the lot was not the hardest aspect to adjust into.

Public and Private Faith

A clear distinction between private and public faith took play: where your worship was either tied to within the threshold of the house, being private and individualized, or over the social public structure of gatherings and feasts, being open and combined.

Public

There are a few records of sites or dwellings of worship in Norse religion. Halls were likely built and used for dual purposes as places of law and festivities as well as rituals and religious sacrifices from the 6th century to well into the Middle Ages.

Religious festivals normally fell around the time when other practices occurred as well, like *things*. "Things" were the gatherings of free people in the community and presided over by law speakers. The gathering occurred in thingsteads and their main function was to counsel and talk over certain major aspects concerned at the time. Kings and chiefs played a central role in the ritualistic practice of public acts and sacrifices presiding and judging accordingly.

Holy rituals were usually located in very specific places associated with the gods and divine forces connected to them. For instance, sacred groves were found to be places where people left offerings in streams and placed them under rocks or in trees to please the landvættir, who were the spirits of the land. It is basically understood that their public faith was rather nature-oriented and the connection to the world around them was their way of reaching to the divine.

Private

It is still unclear whether there was a complete distinction between the private and personal faith performed within the threshold of a Norse family or if it was somehow integrated with that of their public faith.

Usually, it is thought that the head of the household leads the rituals and also chose whether the thrall (slaves) participated in them as well. These were connected to daily tasks instead of seasons or major calendar events.

Rites of passage were extremely important, symbolizing the change of status in personal life, such as becoming a mother, getting married, or dying. When a child is born, it was believed that the fates or Norns would reveal the örlögs of the child as well as the name. This was most often accompanied by prayers to the goddesses Freyja and Frigg to protect and bring well-being over the newborn. Names given were connected to the traits that were seen from the parents or sorceress who assisted in the birthing process.

Marriage was also considered to be a solid center of Scandinavian religion and culture. The important transition for the couple and their respective families would either elevate their status or their legacy. It was necessary that a dowry be presented from the groom's family to that of the future bride and it was a staged ritual of some weeks.

Even though surely most marriages were decided for wealth and social standing, not thinking too much about the happiness and compatibility of the couple, this was actually quite important too, for the couple had to be able to run a farm and family together and, therefore, get along.

Death & Reincarnation

It was very costly to bury a member of the community. If the practices were to be done right, it could take time and money to prepare and properly finalize. Therefore the physical evidence we see today mainly shows boat graves ornately buried along with the person who was most likely elite or royalty of some sorts. We are not too sure what would have happened to commoners (those who didn't fight battles) when they died, as grave sites are far and few, therefore pointing towards probable cremation.

It is unsure where each person's soul would stay within the grave, haunt the home, or join the gods in their realms.

Parts of the Soul

The concept of souls for the Norse was quite different from what we understand today. According to the Norse the soul was divided into four parts:

- **Hamr** was one's physical appearance. It could change and was associated with shapeshifting.
- **Hugr** was the person's character and personality which followed them after death.
- **Fylgja** was their companion animal that reflected their *hugr*. Stronger individuals had stronger totems.
- **Hamingja** was the person's success in life formed by the *hugr* and would be passed down to close family members, either in good or bad omen.

The soul would split after death and each of the four aspects venture into different directions. This was not controlled by the will of the gods and it seemed to be something more personal; therefore, less information is known about it. The *hugr* is what is thought to be what passed onto a newborn baby in the community, and thus the person's character would show itself in the newborn.

The Afterlife

As with most historical sources from the time, they were heavily influenced by Christian writings, but what we do know from the scripts is a general overview of the destination of the souls:

- **Valhalla**: known as the hall of heroes or Odin's hall. Here the warriors of both men and women would meet like old friends to drink, celebrate, and fight in preparation for Ragnarök.
- **Folkvangr**: this is the field of the people watched over by the fertility goddess Freyja. It was the land of peace and rest.
- **Hel**: situated in the ice world of Niflheim and presided over by the goddess Hel, most people went here after death. Most likely a post-Christian adaptation of the underworld as this was not a concept shown before the conversion.
- **Realm of Rán**: also called the Coral Caves of Rán, this giantess would watch over the treasure and sailors befallen to the seas.

- **The Burial Mound**: some souls never left their graves. If they were prepared correctly with all of their treasures and belongings, they would stay in that vicinity and were known as ghosts.

Ghosts

In Norse literature, we see two types of ghosts: the *haugbui* and the *draugr*. These powerful supernatural beings would guard their former possessions and haunt their community.

The haugbui was relatively harmless unless his burial mound was disturbed and deeply attached to places that were comforting to them when they were alive. Some were buried with an open grave-door so that their relatives could bring food offerings, as the dead were known to always be hungry. The draugr, on the other hand, was the more malevolent ghost who haunted their family if they died in bad circumstances or were not buried properly. Some stories say they would wreak havoc in the village by killing animals and destroying property.

Sacrifice

The ritual of sacrifice stood as another central aspect of Norse religion. The Old Norse term *blót* was used to signify the practice, and it was technically an exchange to stay on good terms with their gods. Sacrificing for good weather, luck in battle, and fertility were the most common reasons, but this was also seen at weddings, burials, and birth rights.

Historians believe that there were four fixed sacrifices a year: winter solstice, spring equinox, summer solstice, and the autumn equinox. These were presided over by the magnate or chieftain and accompanied by sorceresses like the völva or the *seiðkona* as a further connection to the deities.

The act of sacrificing an animal to the gods was the central focus of large calendar events. Eating the meat of the sacrificed animal while drinking mead of beer around the fire would bring positive omens to the village and people.

From Snorri's *Hakon* in the *God's Saga* written in the 12th century, we can get a better look at what it entailed and what it meant.

Like his father, Sigurd Hakonsson made sacrifices frequently in their village temple. All sorts of animals were sacrificed, although horses were especially used. The blood of the sacrificed animal was used to spatter on alters, walls, and the participants. The meat that was cooked and eaten by all in attendance and the beer filled was always blessed by the magnate, their pagan priest. Many toasts were then made, one to honor the god Odin, "to the king and victory," and the other to Njörd and Frey, where the cups would be emptied securing a peaceful future. Each person then emptied their cups while pledging to undertake great exploits, and finally was the toast for the dead who rested in their burial mounds.

Not only animals or humans were sacrificed, but weapons and objects of special meaning to the owner were thrown into lakes or rivers. The same sites were frequently used, believing there to be a strong connection to god in that specific location. Sacrificing to statues in forests and groves or in the cult buildings at the center of villages was a common practice too.

There have been a number of disagreements whether human sacrifices were performed during the Viking Age. With the look at some of the sagas we can see the description of human sacrifices of thralls (slaves) in ritualistic practices at funerals, maybe entailing that the free man who owned the thrall would be buried along with him. Some remains in temples suggest ritualistic sacrifice of commanders of war bands consecrating enemy warriors to Odin. And other accounts tell us about hanging the sacrifices by trees along with animals like dogs and cats. Christian propaganda influenced the many stories and sagas we see today, therefore it is unsure if that was the actual truth.

Chapter 8: Connection to Nature & the Unseen

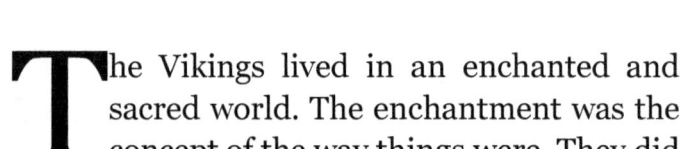

The Vikings lived in an enchanted and sacred world. The enchantment was the concept of the way things were. They did not isolate nature from culture but accepted it fully as they found it, understanding the way it was and how it should be.

They worked on sacramental traditions rather than what we know today as moral religiosity. The divine was found in advancing their interests within the world rather than fundamentally changing its character. After all, they believed that events unfolded by fate and thus were completely out of their control.

Paul Tillich, a twentieth century philosopher of religion, explained their romantic-conservatism as such:

The word 'romantic' in this context, points to the experience of the infinite in the finite, as it is given in nature and history. The word 'conservative' in connection with romance emphasized the experience of the presence of the ultimate in the existing forms of nature and history. If a man sees the holy in the flowers as it grows, in the animal as it moves, in man as he represents a unique individuality, in a special nation, a special culture, a special social system, he is romantic-conservative. For him the given is holy and is the content of his ultimate concern. (McCoy, 2019e)

Their Concepts

We can describe the many different realistic concepts that drove the Norse on their daily journey through Scandinavia, so here we would like to bring to your attention some of the most obvious aspects.

Cyclical View of Time

Unlike our idea of time being linear with a past, present, and future, the Norse saw the past as being just as alive and relatable as their present, therefore cyclical. Time was layered and complex, with the past still continuing to shape their futures and their futures being a debt to be paid (known as skuld) for their actions or lack thereof. There was an importance of fulfilling debt and keeping obligations.

In Sweden, for instance, they would hold a festival called the Great Disting every eight years in the halls at Uppsala:

> This eight year cycle is known as the octa eteris meaning that the moon cycle would return back to the exact same place relative to the sky years prior. This occurred every nine lunar years, a number sacred to their people. (Burton, 2018)

Scandinavians lived so far north that it was impossible to relate to the European times established. Winter days were very short and summer nights even shorter. They divided their days into eight equal parts. They would use daymarks (dagmarks) which were the directions of the sun in the horizon. Their horizon was sectioned into eight parts: north, northeast, east, southeast, south, southwest, west, and northwest. Noon was the most important daymark of the day, when the sun was at its highest. Known as Middag (midday), it marked the midpoint of the sun's path across the horizon.

Geographical location of the sun would change during the year, but the midday point was always in the same place. Mountains were used as identifiers of the midday mark, and many are named after it, like Middagshorn or Hadegisbrekkur (highday). Other landmarks used were fields, bridges, and mountain passes. The closer to the Arctic Circle, the easier it was to establish midday and midnight. Midnight was seen by the slight luminescence of the sun just below the horizon, so one could establish midnight if the sun was due north and midday if the sun was due south.

Herbs and Potions

Archaeobotany has brought up some very interesting findings when it came to the use of plants for healing and magic. The Norse used different plants to remove infection or pain, or a combination of poisonous plants and alcoholic meads that would allow the person to slip into a trance and remove themselves from their physical body to connect to the spirit realm. Each god had an herb that was connected to their theme, which would allow one to interact with this deity when the plant was used for healing, cooking, or potions, called the magical union.

Here are some of the most common plants used at the time:

- Henbane was used in smoking or drinking, which activated its extremely toxic properties, assisting in the arrival of a trance like state.
- Mugwort was used as a diuretic in the household and in rituals for divination.
- Bog Myrtle or Sweet Gale was used as a flavoring additive to many brews and as an antiseptic ointment.
- Meadowsweet was used as a cure for headaches or to reduce indigestion.
- The Elm plant was used as a magical connection to the Alfheim realm and to

carry love spells and other charms into the afterworld.

Many other plants were used in conjunction with rituals as well as their household use. Some connected to the dead and ancestors, and some to love and the living.

Sacred Numbers

In paganism, numbers were often recycled to keep their relevance in each story told. In the Norse mythology we see the numbers three and nine. These numbers reflect in the *Poetic Edda* and in the Icelandic Sagas.

The number three is portrayed in many ways:

- Ymir, Búri, and the cow, Audhumla, are the three original beings.
- There are three Norns.
- There are three sacred wells.
- Before Ragnarök has its time, three long winters will ensue.
- Odin sacrificed himself three times at the Yggdrasil tree in search of the runes.
- Many of the sacred possessions of the gods come in three.

The number nine is portrayed in many ways as well:

- There are nine worlds supported by Yggdrasil.
- Odin hangs from the branches of Yggdrasil for nine days and nights.
- The nine mothers of Heimdallr.
- The great feast and sacrifice in Uppsala occurs every nine years.
- Odin's golden ring Draupnir releases nine golden drops every nine nights.
- Freyr is required to wait nine nights before he can consummate his love for giantess Gerðr.

Spirit Worlds

Wights

Landvættir were the spirits and wights of the land and the natural places surrounding Iceland.

People would often worship and ask for advice in rocks, woods, and waterfalls, as the wights controlled the life of the land, its fertility, and health. Some stories implied that they were already there before the Norse settled, like in the Saga of King Olaf Tryggvason in the *Heimskringla*. King Harald Bluetooth wanted to invade Iceland but before he could, he needed a wizard to send out his spirit to scout for locations where it would be easy to infiltrate the land.

The wizard sent his spirit out in the form of a whale, and while swimming around the northern coasts towards Vopnafjörour, he was confronted by a great dragon named Dreki who was followed by many poisonous snakes, lizards, and insects. So he ventured instead west towards Eyjafjörour, and swimming inland he was met by a huge eagle called Gammur, with wings spanning hillsides, followed by many other birds, deterring him to a new course once again. This time he decided to go south from the west coast into Breioafjörour and was confronted by a bull so horrible and large who called himself Grioungur, and many other landvættir followed behind him. He finally attempted the last region south in Reykjanes where he encountered a giant named Bergrisi who was taller than hills and carried an iron staff. This giant was followed by many other jötnars and, therefore, the wizard had to move away at last. It was established that no longships could sail to Iceland as nothing but wasteland and high crashing waves were enveloping the land.

This story shines through till today in Icelandic culture, traditionally dividing the region into four quarters guarded by these landvættir. You can see them on the coat of arms as well.

Útiseta

This was a practice of clarity, where sitting out the night on crossways was not only for invoking spirits and deities to reveal secrets or counsel, but also to meditate and prepare one's energy for other more strenuous practices later.

It required sitting in darkness in nature, covered in a cloak or blanket, and fasting for many days, as Útiseta means "powering down" or "the act of sitting out" to provoke spirits. The communication received from the outside, such as sounds, smells, and feelings were what grounded the person and clarified their minds so they may hear the spirits around them. The encounter between pupil and spiritual teacher was the goal, looking for answers in the wilderness within and without. Depending on the knowledge you seek, you would invoke the assistance of Odin, Freyja, or Thor.

Here is a passage from the epic Finnish poem *The Kalevala* of a völva's journey through Útiseta:

> Many runes the cold has taught me, many lays the rain has brought me, other songs the winds have sung me. Many birds from many forests, oft have sung me lays in concord, waves of sea and ocean billows, music from the whole creation, oft have been my guide and master. (p. 281)

Totemism

The Norse Kingdoms frequently partook in the practice of totemism. This is the spiritual relationship between humans and different types of animals or plants. The totem is considered the guardian or ancestor of the human whom it is connected to and overlaps the human self—meaning that if the owner died, so did the totem.

Before Christianization, their worldview of this state of being and connection to the natural world was separated into two factions, as explained below.

The Fylgjur

These were the personal animal spirits of individuals assigned to them at birth. *Fylgjur* means 'follower' in Old Norse; therefore, we can understand it as a companion that has a direct correlation to the health of the owner.

The sagas talk about animals such as cats, dogs, foxes, wolves, birds of prey, and mice. Each person's character will be affected by the inherent character of the animal they are connected to. The character of a leader would have the untamed nature of the fox, deer, eagle, or lion, whereas the tame nature of a woman for example would be that of a boar, ox, or goat. If you were of noble descent, it was a bear; if you were of a violent person, it was a wolf, and so on.

Gods were often associated with their own totems, like Odin's ravens or Freyr's boars that would guide and assist them through their adventures.

The animal was known to come to them in dreams and offer advice and what future events are to come. Just like the fates, they were not changeable nor could they act on their own. Sometimes a fylgjur, in the form of a woman, would appear in their dreams. This was known as a *dís*, who was not necessarily the totem, but the goddess attached to their fates telling them what is to come.

Militaristic Totemism

During raids and military action, many men would group up in their group totems of victory, usually a wolf or a bear.

The initiation period required one to go out into the wilderness alone for some time and hunt or scavenge from neighboring villages, imitating the totem they would accept. This implied the need to cleanse both physically and morally before battle.

When the warrior progressed to the next stage of transition it would be that of identification. So the person would often just burst out in a rage of ferocity and savagery. This was fitting into their fylgjur spirit when the men would wear the pelts of the animals and transform into their totems, in a way of shapeshifting their spirits in a symbolic manner.

Numerous sagas tell of warrior shapeshifting into a bear or wolf before battle. For instance, in the saga of the Völsungs, the hero known as Sigmund trains his apprentice Sinfjötli as they wear wolf pelts and become the wolves themselves, raging through the forest. They are known as *ulfhednar,* or "wolf-hides," taking full animalistic behaviors just like the Berserkers (bear-shirts), who were the warrior groups who wore bear and wolf pelts to give them courage and fearlessness in battle.

Chapter 9: Norse Morality & Ethics

More than what was portrayed, the Norse people abided by certain morals and codes of conduct that ruled their lives and whole existence. Let us take a better look at these various structures.

Law

Kings and chiefs played a central role in the ritualistic practice of public acts and meetings. A *thing* was a gathering of various clans and villages, and the law meetings in halls were presided over by the law speakers. Law speakers had to memorize the *Bjarke* law, which regarded smaller merchant towns. A group of Þing, who were free men and women from the villages, often voted and gave a say in these gatherings, whether criminal or political.

Later in the 11th century, especially in Iceland, law became written text. Depending on the Nordic country, criminal proceedings were addressed slightly differently. Punishment most often included fines and, depending on the severity, outlawing, which meant you were no longer protected by the law and therefore capable of receiving any kind of punishment seen fit, something like village justice. Stealing, murdering, raping free women, and even lying and cheating were concerns brought forward to the earls and leaders of the regions for evaluation.

After the influence of Christianity, the proceedings altered and became more civilized. Slavery was abolished and many painful pagan trials to establish innocence were later abolished too.

Virtues and Values

Family was a central part of Norse culture. The ideals behind marriage, children, and raising a good farm to support you your whole life was the goal, originating from the heathen ideals of the *Ásaturu*.

It is unfortunate that the movies, books, and series these days portray an idea of bloodthirsty savagery with no inner values and peaceful practices. This is wrong as it is known from the *Hávamál* poem in the *Codex Regius* as the ethical code of conduct manual for Viking people:

- Courage: More than just being brave in battle, courage was the ideal of living up to the code and standing your ground when defending your beliefs.
- Truth: Lying was considered cowardice, therefore already breaking the first value: to stay true to who you were and what your heart told you was right.
- Honor: Without honor, one could not be courageous or trustworthy. It all fell in line with their personal integrity and dignity.
- Fidelity: More than just the fidelity to their gods and chiefs, it was especially true towards their family and friends.
- Discipline: their total way of life. No matter the environment or situation, one must practice a great deal of self-

discipline to stay true to their virtues and principles.
- Hospitality: also known as the golden rule. Due to the insularity of the visitor being human or a god in disguise, they would offer it because that was the right way.
- Industriousness: Mediocre was not an accepted word for them. You worked your due till it was done with the best interests and full attention.
- Self-reliance: Being extremely independent and frugal for winter months, they strived on having the option to rely on their own thoughts, own families, and own land.
- Perseverance: Finally, to achieve all the above virtues, one needed perseverance. To push and fight through struggles and challenges was what made everything worthwhile.

After Conversion

Some Icelanders and many other Nordic Kingdoms rejected the conversion and began performing *Launblót* (secret offering) to their old gods.

As we have discussed previously, the Viking Age was a time of conversion. Scandinavian people were slowly but surely renouncing their pagan gods. This can be seen archaeologically through the fact that many of the newer graves were lacking grave goods because the converters were buried in standard empty graves.

The conversion was not as hard as it may have seemed. Due to their polytheistic view of gods, accepting a new one into their worldview was not a big challenge. Many of the base values of the Vikings, like plundering, having multiple wives, and engaging in blood feuds, never really changed after their conversion. It seems they really didn't care whether they were going to Heaven or Valhalla, as long as they lived free and favorably.

Christianity tainted the reality of the course of history through their divine eyes, and we struggle to see beyond that due to the lack of original written information. The kings and rulers of greater European regions benefited from the top to bottom conversion, so they were able to use the power of northerner's. The Norse people themselves benefited from the bottom-up conversion, so they could socially evolve and become a stronger nation for it. Baptism was pushed by English Kings onto their Viking leaders who were defeated, not necessarily for the savior of their souls, but for the forced peace that would come of it.

"Ironically, more Norse would be forced into Christian conversion by Vikings than by the kings of Christendom" (Sons of Vikings, 2019).

Conclusion

——⟨⋈⟩——

The night is cold and silent. A breeze of snowy wind moves through the mountain pass and encircles Arne and his son as they climb up the same route that has been used for almost a century now.

Arne has grown into a strong and reliable member of his community and now, in turn, takes his young son Frode up the pass to that clearing where he and his own father, Bo, came many moons before. This tradition has stayed firm and true in their family, so that he may be able to tell the same stories and legends that brought him closer to his ancestors and gods. Now that his own son has reached the right age to join him on this trip, it marks a new beginning to manhood and maturity, and it makes Arne very proud.

As they reach the same clearing between the two Ash trees that have been standing vigil there for as long as he can remember, they quietly look up into the night sky and marvel once more at the performance above their heads. Arne looks at the childlike bewilderment in his son's face and remembers his own excitement when taking the trip and seeing the colors dance in front of him. But he also gets a sense of melancholy for the changes that are happening around them and which he cannot stop.

The stories that are told today are still the same, but Arne knows that another influence is making its way into their lives and culture as a whole. Many priests have come through his village to spread the word of this new god and many of his friends have argued about it around the fires. Arne has had his doubts for years, but still chooses to hold a firm belief in his own gods and their might and allow his family to talk and worship their magic just the same.

Even though he joined many ventures to the lands of the east for trade, he still prefers his freedom here in the place he calls home. His cousins have told him of their raids and riches in the west, but nothing will keep him from his farm and traditions. He will never say this out loud, but he is afraid of the change, and where many seem excited and eager to forget their old ways, he will not. That is why he takes his son up the pass, so that no matter what Frode chooses in his own adult life, he always remembers the stories and songs that make them the men of the north.

The winds of change will not reach them here, in their cold wilderness, under the watchful eyes of their gods, so he quietly begins his tales as his son watches on.

Farewell

Well, there you have it, dear reader and lover of ancient things!

The condensation of historical and cultural content has been broken down for you to be able to return to whenever you need to remember the old ways. We believe that history can always teach a person something new, whether it is for practical and educational purposes or for the knowledge of something deeper within. We are hopeful that you are reading this conclusion with a broader understanding of Norse magic and its surrounding myth. With a smile and an open heart, we thank you for choosing this piece of literature to expand your own ideals, thoughts on their history, and the influences their 600 years of existence have had on the world.

We would have you take a minute to realize just how the Norse were so attuned to another dimensional consciousness and how we can take something from that and mold it into our own busy and noisy world. Whether you were simply hungry for the information and wanted to understand this mysterious culture or you were beginning to master the heathen arts, then you have received some valuable information from this precious book. By bringing to you the modalities of their life, we hope you can take this book and apply it to your inner search for happiness, truth, and the connection to your Wyrd.

We touched on the lives of the common farmers and their practice of paganism with regards to family and surrounding communities. Then we pressed on to their warriors, the Vikings, that made fame and fortune from war and trade which left a lasting mark on the world around them. Touching on their gods and goddesses and the countless worlds which they inhabit, we were then able to take you on the journey through their mythologies and folktales written by pagans and Christians alike. We loved telling you about their magic and witchcraft and their innate need for answers and guidance from the unseen world. We discussed their use of the markings that you now know to be more than just a language but a means to conjure and manipulate the magical world around them. Then, we broke down how you can start practicing this divination in your own capacity through the runes. Towards the final chapters, we spoke about their spiritual connection to nature and the animals and plants that live within it, to lastly touch on their concepts of honor, valor, hospitality, and the heavy influence of the new god that tamed them and brought an end to their savage ways.

Thank you again for your enthusiasm and interest in a subject that is so intriguing and raw. It resonates with a deeper consciousness that we might have lost many centuries ago, but that can be found again if we decide to listen to the songs and watch for the signs that are all around us.

Free Bonus from HBA: Ebook Bundle

Greetings!

First of all, thank you for reading our books. As fellow passionate readers of history and mythology we aim to create the very best books for our readers.

Now, we invite you to join our VIP list. As a welcome gift we offer the History & Mythology Ebook Bundle below for free. Plus you can be the first to receive new books and exclusives! Remember it's 100% free to join.

Simply click the link below to join.

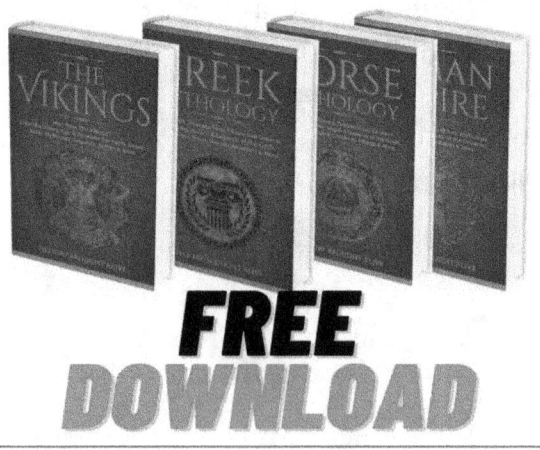

Click Here For Your Free Bonus (https://www.subscribepage.com/hba)

Keep upto date with us on:
YouTube: History Brought Alive
Facebook: History Brought Alive
www.historybroughtalive.com

References

Absolute History. (2021, June 29). *The untold legends of female Vikings who conquered Iceland | Viking women | Absolute History* [Video]. YouTube. https://www.youtube.com/watch?v=9orVsF0pZ1U

Adrien, C. J. (2021). *What was the difference between Danish, Norwegian, Swedish Vikings?* C.J Adrien. https://cjadrien.com/difference-danish-norwegian-swedish-vikings/

Arctic Adventures. (2021). *Icelandic sagas | What makes them so interesting?* Arctic Adventures. https://adventures.is/information/icelandic-sagas/

Auntyflo. (2021). *Rune the unknowable.* Auntyflo.com. https://www.auntyflo.com/rune-stones/rune-unknowable

Britannica. (2019). *Denmark - The Viking era.* Encyclopædia Britannica.

https://www.britannica.com/place/Denmark/The-Viking-era

Burton, T. (2018, April 10). *The Anglo-Norse concept of time.* Medium. https://medium.com/@thomburton/the-anglo-norse-concept-of-time-a6aee671ae36

Carter, R. (2020, December 8). *11 Creatures from Scandinavian folklore you should know.* Scandification. https://scandification.com/scandinavian-folklore-creatures/

Crawford, J. [Jackson Crawford]. (2017, June 5). *Writing English in Runes* [Video]. YouTube. https://www.youtube.com/watch?v=A271ohcO7Yc

Crawford, J. [Jackson Crawford]. (2021, May 18). *Poetic of Edda.* YouTube. https://www.youtube.com/watch?v=nbi9mQCRd18&t=454s

Creepyhollows. (2021). *How-to read runes.* Instructables. https://www.instructables.com/How-To-Read-Runes/

Dashu, M. (2016). *Witches and pagans: Women in European folk religion, 700-1100*. Velona Press. (Original work published 2014).

Devereaux, L. (2019, February 7). *Scandinavian time measurement during the Viking era*. The Falcon Banner. http://falconbanner.gladiusinfractus.com/2019/02/07/scandinavian-time-measurement-during-the-viking-era/

Fotevikens Museum. (2016). *Agricultural plants in the Viking*. Fotevikens Museum. https://www.fotevikensmuseum.se/d/en/vikingar/hur/mat/recept/vaxter

Germanic Mythology. (2021). *Grímnismál: Texts and translations*. http://www.germanicmythology.com/PoeticEdda/GRMThorpe.html

Goodrich, R. (2018, August 29). *Viking history: Facts & myths*. Live Science. https://www.livescience.com/32087-viking-history-facts-myths.html

Grimfrost. (2020a, October 3). *Grimfrost Academy: Viking age herbs in food, culture and magic* [Video]. YouTube. https://www.youtube.com/watch?v=mhMHTZ2jfXM

Grimfrost. (2020b). *Grimfrost Academy - Viking religion* [Video]. YouTube. https://www.youtube.com/watch?v=ruQw7ieoGJM

Groeneveld, E. (2017, November 2). *Norse Mythology*. World History Encyclopedia. https://www.worldhistory.org/Norse_Mythology/

Gronitz, D. (2021). *The Rune Site | Casting layouts and spreads*. The Runesite. http://www.therunesite.com/casting-layouts-and-spreads/

Guido. (n.d.). *Chapter 10: The Ætt in rune casting*. Mind Unfolded. https://sites.google.com/site/mindunfolded/chapter-6

Gundarsson, K. (2021). *Space-Craft, seiðr, and shamanism*. Hrafnar.org. https://hrafnar.org/articles/kveldulf/spaecraft/

Hanson, M. (2016, October 27). *Norse mythology*. English History.

https://englishhistory.net/vikings/norse-mythology/

Harger, A. (2021, June 30). *Rune divination methods: Introduction* [Video]. YouTube. https://www.youtube.com/watch?v=jJNSfzZuTu0

Harlitz-Kern, E. (2019, October 24). *12 Surprising facts about Viking runestones*. Mental Floss. https://www.mentalfloss.com/article/601594/viking-runestone-facts

History Extra. (2015, April 8). *Top 10 Viking stories*. HistoryExtra. https://www.historyextra.com/period/viking/top-10-viking-stories/

History on the Net. (2018, May 29). *Viking runes and runestones - History*. History. https://www.historyonthenet.com/viking-runes-and-runestones

History.com Editors. (2018, August 21). *Vikings*. History. https://www.history.com/topics/exploration/vikings-history

Iceland Rovers. (2017, January 5). *Mythology of Iceland - The Magical Staves -*

Icelandic sagas. Iceland Rovers. https://www.icelandrovers.is/blog/the-magical-staves-of-iceland/

Icelandic Literature Center. (n.d.). *The Edda & the Sagas of the Icelanders.* https://www.islit.is/en/promotion-and-translations/icelandic-literature/the-edda-and-the-sagas-of-the-icelanders/

J. Mark, J. (2018a, December 10). *Norse ghosts & the afterlife.* World History Encyclopedia. https://www.worldhistory.org/article/1290/norse-ghosts--the-afterlife/#:~:text=There%20is%20evidence%20that%20the

J. Mark, J. (2018b, December 20). *Nine Realms of Norse Cosmology.* World History Encyclopedia. https://www.worldhistory.org/article/1305/nine-realms-of-norse-cosmology/

Kneale, A. (2013, July 20). *Celts and Vikings - Scandinavian influences on the Celtic nations.* Transceltic. https://www.transceltic.com/pan-celtic/celts-and-vikings-scandinavian-influences-celtic-nations

Lin, K. (2017, March 21). *Edda*. World History Encyclopedia. https://www.worldhistory.org/Edda/

McCoy, D. (2009). *Loki - Norse Mythology for smart people.* Norse Mythology. https://norse-mythology.org/gods-and-creatures/the-aesir-gods-and-goddesses/loki/

McCoy, D. (2012a). *Baldur - Norse Mythology for smart people.* Norse Mythology. https://norse-mythology.org/gods-and-creatures/the-aesir-gods-and-goddesses/baldur/

McCoy, D. (2012b). *Freyr - Norse Mythology for smart people.* Norse Mythology. https://norse-mythology.org/gods-and-creatures/the-vanir-gods-and-goddesses/freyr/

McCoy, D. (2012c). *Njord - Norse Mythology for smart people.* Norse Mythology. https://norse-mythology.org/gods-and-creatures/the-vanir-gods-and-goddesses/njord/

McCoy, D. (2012d). *Odin - Norse Mythology for Smart People.* Norse Mythology for Smart People. https://norse-mythology.org/gods-and-creatures/the-aesir-gods-and-goddesses/odin/

McCoy, D. (2012e). *Ragnarok - Norse Mythology for smart people*. Norse Mythology. https://norse-mythology.org/tales/ragnarok/

McCoy, D. (2012f). *Valkyries - Norse Mythology for smart people*. Norse Mythology. https://norse-mythology.org/gods-and-creatures/valkyries/

McCoy, D. (2019a). *Elves - Norse Mythology for smart people*. Norse Mythology. https://norse-mythology.org/gods-and-creatures/elves/

McCoy, D. (2019b). *Forseti - Norse Mythology for smart people*. Norse Mythology. https://norse-mythology.org/forseti/

McCoy, D. (2019c). *Odin's discovery of the runes*. Norse Mythology. https://norse-mythology.org/tales/odins-discovery-of-the-runes/

McCoy, D. (2019d). *Seidr*. Norse Mythology. https://norse-mythology.org/concepts/seidr/

McCoy, D. (2019e). *The enchanted world.* Norse Mythology. https://norse-mythology.org/the-enchanted-world/

McCoy, D. (2019f). *The kidnapping of Idun.* Norse Mythology. https://norse-mythology.org/tales/the-kidnapping-of-idun/

McCoy, D. (2019g). *Totemism.* Norse Mythology. https://norse-mythology.org/concepts/totemism/

McCoy, D. (2021). *The Aesir-Vanir War.* Norse Mythology. https://norse-mythology.org/tales/the-aesir-vanir-war/

Newcombe, R. (2019). *Rune guide - An introduction to using the runes.* Holistic Shop. https://www.holisticshop.co.uk/articles/guide-runes

Nikel, D. (2020, April 29). *Norwegian mythology & folk tales.* Life in Norway. https://www.lifeinnorway.net/norwegian-mythology-folk-tales/

Norse Magic and Beliefs. (2021, February 27). *The different types of Norse magic* [Video]. YouTube.

https://www.youtube.com/watch?v=VAY6ai4pzvk&t=157s

Raging Seas Blog. (n.d.). *Norse magic: A simplified introduction* [Tumblr post]. Tumblr. https://ragingseas.tumblr.com/post/172717314664/norse-magic-a-simplified-introduction

Personified. (2014, August 16). *Spae-craft & Seidr - Magic forums.* SpellsOfMagic. https://www.spellsofmagic.com/read_post.html?post=666296

Rune, M. (2014, September 13). *Path of the Valkyries.* Novel Ideas. https://www.miriamrune.co.uk/path-of-the-valkyries/

Salvör, B. (n.d.). *A guide to Icelandic runes.* Guide to Iceland. https://guidetoiceland.is/history-culture/a-guide-to-icelandic-runes

Sandra, B. (2016, October 29). *Pesta: The personification of the Black Plague in Norway.* Myths and Microbes. https://mythsandmicrobes.com/2016/09/29/pesta-the-personification-of-the-black-plague-in-norway/

Schellenberg, J. (2015, November 16). *A Viking love story*. Europeana Foundation. https://www.europeana.eu/en/blog/a-viking-love-story-the-saga-of-frithiof

Shweta. (2019, May 29). *The concept of love in Norse mythology*. Scoopify. https://www.scoopify.org/the-concept-of-love-in-norse-mythology/

Sons Of Vikings. (2019, March 26). *Vikings and religion*. Sons of Vikings. https://sonsofvikings.com/blogs/history/the-vikings-and-christianity

Super User. (2014). *Mythology of the northern lights*. The Aurora Zone. https://www.theaurorazone.com/about-the-aurora/aurora-legends

Talisa + Sam. (n.d.). *Rune meanings and how to use rune stones for divination*. Two Wander. https://www.twowander.com/blog/rune-meanings-how-to-use-runestones-for-divination

TED-Ed. (2020). *The secret messages of Viking runestones - Jesse Byock* [Video]. YouTube.

https://www.youtube.com/watch?v=wOcVy5dvwjs

The Viking Rune. (2019). *Writing in runes — How to start writing in Norse runes.* Viking Rune. https://www.vikingrune.com/2013/09/guide-to-writing-in-runes/

Timeline. (2018, April 1). *How the Norsemen became the seafaring Vikings | Wings Of A Dragon | Timeline* [Video]. YouTube. https://www.youtube.com/watch?v=hOsTfZ8gTM8&t=431s

Tommy. (2021). *What is the relationship between Vikings and Celts?* Herreira. https://harreira.com/viking/what-is-the-relationship-between-vikings-and-celts/

V.K.N.G. (2020, April 6). *Famous Valkyries [Divine Shield maidens].* Norse and Viking Mythology [Best Blog] - Vkngjewelry. https://blog.vkngjewelry.com/en/famous-valkyries/

Viking Archaeology. (2021). *Viking Archaeology - Eddaic Poetry.* Viking.archeurope.info.

http://viking.archeurope.info/index.php?page=eddaic-poetry

Vikings, S. (2020, May 27). *Learning about the Younger Futhark runes* [Video]. YouTube. https://www.youtube.com/watch?v=a6mxX4kYG10

Wanner, K. J. (2008). *Snorri Sturluson and the Edda: The conversion of cultural capital in medieval Scandinavia.* University Of Toronto Press, Cop.

Well… Actually. (2016, January 12). *Runology - The study of runes* [Video]. YouTube. https://www.youtube.com/watch?v=YTdPDBBxK8A

Wikipedia. (2020a, December 6). *Younger Futhark.* Wikipedia. https://en.wikipedia.org/wiki/Younger_Futhark

Wikipedia. (2020b, December 14). *Old Norse poetry.* Wikipedia. https://en.wikipedia.org/wiki/Old_Norse_poetry

Wikipedia. (2021a, March 31). *Saga.* Wikipedia. https://en.wikipedia.org/wiki/Saga

Wikipedia. (2021b, May 27). *Rune poem*. Wikipedia. https://en.wikipedia.org/wiki/Rune_poem

Wikipedia. (2021c, May 31). *Numbers in Norse mythology*. Wikipedia. https://en.wikipedia.org/wiki/Numbers_in_Norse_mythology

Wikipedia. (2021d, June 11). *Galdr*. Wikipedia. https://en.wikipedia.org/wiki/Galdr

Wikipedia. (2021e, June 22). *Settlement of Iceland*. Wikipedia. https://en.wikipedia.org/wiki/Settlement_of_Iceland

Wikipedia. (2021f, July 16). *Nixie (folklore)*. Wikipedia. https://en.wikipedia.org/wiki/Nixie_(folklore)

Wikipedia Contributors. (2019a, September 23). *Medieval Scandinavian law*. Wikipedia. https://en.wikipedia.org/wiki/Medieval_Scandinavian_law

Wikipedia Contributors. (2019b, November 19). *Sagas of Icelanders*. Wikipedia.

https://en.wikipedia.org/wiki/Sagas_of_Icelanders

Wikipedia Contributors. (2021a, March 17). *Frithiof's Saga*. Wikipedia. https://en.wikipedia.org/wiki/Frithiof%27s_Saga

Wikipedia Contributors. (2021b, May 15). *Þorbjörg Lítilvölva*. Wikipedia. https://en.wikipedia.org/wiki/%C3%9Eorbj%C3%B6rg_L%C3%ADtilv%C3%B6lva#cite_note-SEPHTON-1880-12-13-3

Wikipedia Contributors. (2021c, May 17). *Landvættir*. Wikipedia. https://en.wikipedia.org/wiki/Landv%C3%A6ttir

Wikipedia Contributors. (2021d, June 10). *Seiðr*. Wikipedia. https://en.wikipedia.org/wiki/Sei%C3%B0r

Wikipedia Contributors. (2021e, July 11). *Dökkálfar and Ljósálfar*. Wikipedia. https://en.wikipedia.org/wiki/D%C3%B6kk%C3%A1lfar_and_Lj%C3%B3s%C3%A1lfar

www.ingramcontent.com/pod-product-compliance
Lightning Source LLC
Chambersburg PA
CBHW071614080526
44588CB00010B/1128